As one of the world's longest establi[shed]
and best-known travel br[ands],
Thomas Cook are the experts in tr[avel].

For more than 135 years [our]
guidebooks have unlocked the sec[rets]
of destinations around the wo[rld],
sharing with travellers a wealth [of]
experience and a passion for travel.

**Rely on Thomas Cook as your
travelling companion on your next trip
and benefit from our unique heritage.**

Thomas Cook **traveller** guides

MENORCA

Lindsay Bennett

Your travelling companion since 1873

Thomas
Cook

Written by Lindsay Bennett, updated by Josephine Quintero
Original photography by Pete Bennett

Published by Thomas Cook Publishing
A division of Thomas Cook Tour Operations Limited
Company registration no. 3772199 England
The Thomas Cook Business Park, 9 Coningsby Road,
Peterborough PE3 8SB, United Kingdom
Email: books@thomascook.com, Tel: +44 (0) 1733 416477
www.thomascookpublishing.com

Produced by Cambridge Publishing Management Limited
Burr Elm Court, Main Street, Caldecote CB23 7NU
www.cambridgepm.co.uk

ISBN: 978-1-84848-426-9

© 2006, 2008 Thomas Cook Publishing
This third edition © 2011
Text © Thomas Cook Publishing
Maps © Thomas Cook Publishing/PCGraphics (UK) Limited

Series Editor: Karen Beaulah
Production/DTP: Steven Collins

Printed and bound in Spain by GraphyCems

Cover photography: © Nigel Roberson/Alamy

Contents

Introduction

Wall-to-wall sunshine and non-stop partying tend to be the first things people think about when you mention the Balearics. These pretty islands scattered in the western Mediterranean have gained a reputation as the destination where an entire generation of Northern European youth heads to pass a week or two in a haze of hedonistic pleasure while cultivating a deep sun tan to impress their mates back home.

But while this may be partly true of Ibiza and Mallorca, the two most visited islands, you'd be wrong to think Menorca is the same. This is the island that paused to think when the tourist dollars began to roll in, turned its back on the raucous, booze-fuelled clubbing market and took a different direction.

Menorca has deliberately limited its tourist development. After a few early errors, the new development is tasteful and low-rise, in sympathy with the landscape and not working against it. It has marketed itself as 'the family island' but this certainly doesn't exclude the young, the single and those without kids. The warm and relaxed welcome and resort activities are low-key and it is a great place to get active on land or water, on two legs or two wheels, on four legs (equine) or with a scuba tank strapped to your back.

The island's magnificent coastline is its most stunning asset. From rocky inlets to vast stretches of sand, the golden beaches are caressed by azure waters making excellent playgrounds for yachtsmen – and their white-masted vessels anchored offshore only add to the picture-perfect vista. Where the sand stops the limestone begins, its surface eroded into surreal shapes and narrow valleys, and cut by numerous caverns.

Nature's raw material has been in good hands for centuries, sculpted by man since before the Bronze Age. History has cast a long and languorous shadow here, and you can spend more than a day or two clambering among

MAYONNAISE: A CULINARY GIFT TO THE WORLD

Menorca's most famous gift to the world was invented during the French suzerainty of the island. The official version that the sauce was invented by the French chef to the Duke de Richelieu is hotly disputed by the Menorcans who are pretty sure that this chef stole the recipe from a local girl working in the kitchen and called it his own – naming it Mayonnaise or Mahonnaise after the Menorcan capital Mahon, now Maó. Fast food wouldn't be the same without it!

dusty ancient stones or marching to the beat of the military drum of many a colonial army.

For generations the Menorcans have seen powerbrokers from the rest of Europe come and go while working the land and fishing the seas. Ties with the island's tradition are strong even in the face of 21st-century modernity and tourism seems to flow with this tradition rather than crowding it out.

UNESCO recognised the Menorcans' unique relationship with their land in 1993 when they awarded the island the coveted 'biosphere reserve' status. Since then, the Parc Naturel de S'Albufera des Grau has been created and the wetlands lying behind the beach at Son Bou have been granted conservation status. Coastal wetlands at Addaia (*see pp85–6*) and Son Saura (*see p143*) are also under protection. Birdlife is burgeoning, rare grasses and plants are regrowing while butterflies and insects are blooming once more. These carefully cosseted areas are seeing the advent of hikers and nature enthusiasts to add to the beach-bound tourists of recent years.

Introduction

The pretty white houses of Alaior

The island

Menorca is a small island but its geological diversity is impressive. Its relative isolation has led to the preservation of a number of rare species and the development of several species found only here or on the sister Balearic Islands. Menorca can be divided in landscape and climate into north and south, named after the winds that play across the land – the migjorn *of the south and the* tramuntana *of the north.*

The Migjorn (the south)

Menorca's south (*see pp100–115*) is the area that first welcomes the warm southerly winds from Africa. The limestone and sandstone substrate was laid down during the Miocene era; since then, it has been eroded by wind and water into hundreds of steep valleys or *barrancas* ending in narrow inlets that house the island's famous *cala* resorts. The vegetation is much more lush here, sheltered from the winds, with orange and holm oak groves.

The Tramuntana (the north)

The north (*see pp84–99*) offers a totally different landscape with deep inlets and dramatic rock formations. The northerly winds hold sway here and, particularly in winter, they race across the northern Mediterranean at up to 90kph (56mph), hitting the lowlands of Menorca. Here you will find low-growing, 'alpine-type' scrubland and wild olives bent against the prevailing airflow. In some places there is no vegetation at all, and man-made structures like the ancient *talaiots* or the modern *barraques* (stone sheep pens) stand sentinel against the skyline.

The Transition Zone

Where north meets south there is a fertile transition zone where much of the island's farmland can be found. The main cross-country route through the island, the ME1, runs through the heart of this zone, past fields replete with wild flowers in the spring, maize in the summer, and ripening citrus and olives in the autumn.

Biosphere reserve

Menorca joined over 410 locations worldwide when UNESCO declared the whole island a biosphere reserve in 1993 in recognition of the unique relationship between the islanders and the landscape. This acknowledges the efforts made to develop in a sustainable way with respect to the landscape and cultural traditions.

The island

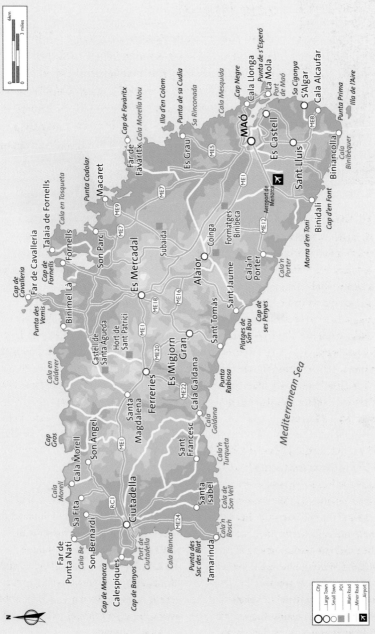

Cap de Cavalleria
Far de Cavalleria
Talaia de Fornells
Cala en Tosqueta
Punta Codolar
Macaret
Cap de Favàritx
Far de Favàritx
Cala Morella Nou
Illa d'en Colom
Punta de sa Cudia
Sa Rinconada
Cala Mesquida
Cap Negre
Cala Llonga
Punta de s'Esperó
La Mola
Port de Maó
Sa Cigonya
S'Algar
Cala Alcaufar
Punta Prima
Illa de l'Aire

Cap de Cavalleria
Cap de Fornells
Fornells
Son Parc
ME9
ME7
Es Mercadal
Es Grau
ME5
MAÓ
Es Castell
Sant Lluís
ME8
Biniancolla
Cala Binibèquer

Punta des Vernis
Binimel·là
ME18
ME16
ME1
Subaida
Alaior
Sant Jaume
Sant Tomàs
Coinga
Formatges Binibeca
ME12
Cala'n Porter
Cala'n Porter
Cap d'en Font
Morra d'en Toni
Binidalí
Aeroport de Menorca

Cap de Cavalleria
Castell de Santa Agueda
Hort de Sant Patrici
ME20
Es Migjorn Gran
ME22
Ferreries
Cala Galdana
Punta Rabiosa
Platges de Son Bou
Cap de ses Penyes

Mediterranean Sea

Cala en Calderer
Santa Magdalena
Sant Francesc
Cala Galdana
Cala'n Turqueta

Cap Gros
Cala Morell
Son Àngel
Son Morell
ME1
Santa Isabel
Cala de Son Vell

Cala Morell
Sa Fita
Son Bernardí
Ciutadella
RC1
ME24
Cala'n Bosch

Far de Punta Nati
Calespiques
Cap de Menorca
Cala Be
Port de Ciutadella
Cala Blanca
Punta des Sac des Blat
Tamarinda
Cap de Banyos

City
Large Town
Small Town
POI
Main Road
Minor Road
Airport

6km
3 miles

UNESCO (*www.unesco.org*) defines biosphere reserves as 'areas of terrestrial and coastal ecosystems promoting solutions to reconcile the conservation of biodiversity with its sustainable use'. Biosphere reserves serve in some way as living laboratories for testing out and demonstrating integrated management of land, water and biodiversity. Each biosphere reserve is intended to fulfil three basic functions, which are complementary and mutually reinforcing:

- A conservation function – to contribute to the conservation of landscapes, ecosystems, species and genetic variation.
- A development function – to foster economic and human development that is culturally and ecologically sustainable.
- A logistic function – to provide support for research, monitoring, education and information exchange related to local, national and global issues of conservation and development.

Environment protection

The Menorcan Council agreed an Island Territorial Plan in 2003 to protect its environment in the coming years, the key points of which were:

- Limiting urban development in key areas, including controlling growth of tourist complexes.
- Implementation of a recycling programme.

- Bringing 60 per cent of the island under protected status.
- Prohibiting building on rural lands.
- Protection of natural native ecosystems by taking steps to eradicate foreign species of plant that have invaded the shores and taken over the native plants.
- Funding research into the history and cultural heritage of the island.

Much progress has been made for these projects: a localised recycling programme is in effect, more land has now acquired protected status and a great deal of success has been had with the reintroduction of native flora and fauna. Cycle paths have been created on old, potholed roads, the Camí des Cavalls (*see p144*) has been restored, ancient sites have been developed, eco-museums have been opened (*see p140*) and the seabeds have been cleaned up. *For further details contact the Consell Insular de Menorca. Tel: 902 35 60 50. www.cime.es*

Flora

Menorca has less diversity than the other Balearic Islands, perhaps because the strong winds stop the propagation of some delicate species. The uncultivated areas offer acres of hardy Mediterranean holm oak and wild olive or oleaster, often bent into bizarre shapes by the wind. Fragrant pines and other evergreens cover tracts of the interior along with the mastic tree that releases a useful resin. In the northern extremities, the rocky headlands are blanketed in low-growing shrubs, wild herbs and sturdy species such as heather, lentisk and box, while each sheltered barranca in the south is its own unique ecosystem. Along some of the more remote beaches it is possible to find wild lilies.

Fauna

Menorca is renowned for its birdlife (*see pp166–7*) with a year-round wealth of predator birds. The other highlight of its fauna is reptiles. The protected offshore islands are home to rare varieties including four species of lizard which are endemic to the Balearics. Three of these may be found on Menorca: Lilford's wall lizard, a black, green and blue lizard, generally found scaling walls; the similarly vibrant olive-green and black striped Italian lizard; and the Moroccan rock lizard; which has olive-green and blue colouring. The Balearic rabbit and the short-legged vole also make an appearance, as does the voracious pine marten and a North African subspecies

A GEOLOGICAL DIVIDE

The bay of Cala Morell (*see pp120–21*) sits astride a geological fault that slices through Menorca. This is most easily seen by the totally different colour and constitution of the rocks on the east and west sides of the bay. A flight of steps has been carved at the site of the fault at the eastern end of the bay.

of hedgehog. There are also four species of harmless snake on the island: the Viperine Snake, Grass Snake, False Smooth Snake and Ladder Snake.

The people

There are just under 88,000 Menorcans, most of whom speak Menorquí, a dialect of Catalan, although signs are a muddle of Catalan and Castilian Spanish. Three-quarters of the island's inhabitants live in Maó and Ciutadella. The Roman Catholic faith is a strong force that binds the community together, and tourism is the economic lifeblood that feeds the comparatively high per capita income of Menorcans when compared with other parts of Spain.

Bathing platforms at Cala'n Bruch

History

c. 4000 BC The earliest evidence of human settlement on the island, but little is known about these people beyond the fact that they were farmers and hunters. Late in this period, caves are used for housing and as ritual sites.

c. 2500 BC The first 'Megalithic' structures begin to be built.

c. 1400 BC Evidence of cross-cultural and technological trade between ancient Menorcans and the Beaker people. The Talayotic era begins around this time.

Early 1st millennium BC Trading contacts are made with the Phoenicians and Greeks.

3rd century BC Carthaginians take the island by force. Their main settlement on the site of today's Maó is called Magón (after Magó, brother of Hannibal), while a settlement on the site of present-day Ciutadella was named Jamma. Later, during the Punic Wars, the Balearic Islands are a valuable Carthaginian base for attacks further east to the heart of Rome; but, as Rome becomes more powerful, Carthage retreats to northern Africa.

123 BC The Romans take the island, giving it the name Minorica.

1st century BC–3rd century AD Stability under Rome, which introduces olive oil and grapes to the island. Port Magonum (Maó) is the administrative capital.

AD 404 The Balearics become a separate Roman province.

420s Vandals arrive and systematically destroy towns and churches.

533 Byzantine forces rout the Vandals and Menorca becomes part of the empire ruled from Constantinople, through feudal chieftains.

8th and 9th centuries Raids by Muslim forces from the north coast of Africa. Byzantine control is loosened.

903 Menorca is taken by Muslim Moors under the control of the Emir of Cordoba.

1015 After the Cordoba regime collapses, the island comes under the influence of the Taifa Muslims at Denia.

1085 The Balearics become an independent Muslim 'emirate'; Christians begin to be persecuted, to the anger of surrounding Catholic nations.

Early 12th century A Norman Christian invasion is repelled by the Muslims.

1116 The Almoravides Muslims take over, starting a period of relative calm.

1203 The Almohad Muslims take custody of the islands.

1229 Jaume I (ruler of Catalonia and Aragon) takes Mallorca by force and, in 1232, Menorca by negotiation. Ciutadella is reinforced as the leading town of the island.

1276 Death of Jaume. Menorca becomes part of the kingdom of Mallorca. The following few years see the island swing between Mallorca and Aragon.

1287 Alfonso III claims the island for Aragon on 17 January, now Menorca's national day.

1344 Pedro of Aragon retakes the island. Jaume III dies trying to recapture his kingdom in 1349.

1348 The Black Death hits the population.

Early 15th century The island is on the verge of civil war with the countryside in revolt against taxes.

1463 A civil war breaks out as the countryside supports Joan II. Ciutadella stays loyal to the king.

1469 The marriage of Isabel of Castile to Fernando of Aragon unites the Spanish under one crown.

1535 The Ottomans arrive in the Balearics. Maó is sacked by Barbarossa and Castell Sant Felip is built to protect the harbour; many Menorcans are taken into slavery.

1558	Ciutadella falls into Turkish hands in what was to become 'the year of misfortune'.
1627	Ciutadella is forced to relinquish some of its administrative control to other towns on the island.
1706	The vacant throne of Spain results in the pan-European Spanish War of Succession. The island's population is split between the two opposing camps of Archduke Carlos and Philip of Anjou. Philip takes the crown.
1708	Britain takes Menorca for the first time, ostensibly in support of Carlos but actually to gain control of what has become a major Mediterranean port.
1713	The Treaty of Utrecht concludes the Spanish War of Succession. It also affirms Britain's territorial right to Menorca.
1722	Maó becomes the island's capital, and a British naval base.
1756	The French take Menorca during the Seven Years War. They build the town of Sant Lluís.
1763	The British return to Menorca.
1782	Charles III of Spain takes Menorca in a combined Franco-Spanish offensive. Fort St Phillip is destroyed.
1798	The British return for the final time, taking control during the Napoleonic Wars.
1802	Menorca is formally given over to Spanish rule under the Treaty of Amiens. Castilian becomes Spain's official language and the Catalan spoken on the islands a secondary language.
1820	The Menorcan economy collapses due to a ban on movement of cereals. Mass migration to North Africa.
1830	After the French take Algiers, more Menorcans leave the island to set up home there.
1850	The first footwear factories are founded in Ciutadella.

1860	Isabel II, Queen of Spain, visits the new fortifications at La Mola – the fort is named in her honour.
Late 19th and early 20th centuries	The footwear industry stalls as a major market, Cuba, becomes independent. Another wave of migration, this time to the USA, sees Menorca's population drop.
1936–9	The Spanish Civil War rends the country in two. Menorca remains loyal to the existing republic but much bloodshed is prevented by a negotiated surrender.
1939–75	The Catalan language is repressed by Franco. Mainland Spaniards move to the island, mixing the population for the first time in many years.
1950s	The first seeds of mass tourism are sown.
1975	Death of Franco and reinstatement of the Spanish monarchy as part of a parliamentary democratic constitution.
1983	The Balearics (Formentera, Ibiza, Mallorca and Menorca) become a semi-autonomous region in a reorganisation of the Spanish system. The Menorcan Island Council is inaugurated, giving the population limited self-determination.
1986	Spain joins the precursor of today's EU, the European Community.
1993	Menorca is awarded the Biosphere Reserve title by UNESCO under its programme 'Man and Landscape'.
Late 20th century	Catalan once again becomes the official language.
2004	Menorca remains staunchly Conservative as Socialists sweep to power in Madrid, in the wake of the Al Qaeda bombings.
2005	The island's application to become the 25th member of the International Island Games Association is approved.
2009	Menorca takes part in the Island Games, a biennial athletic competition between teams from islands and other small territories.

The House of Aragon

More complicated than the plot of any soap opera, the history of the House of Aragon includes more than a few murders, illegitimate births, family fallouts and religious wars. Much of what we call Spain and southern France was the domain of three sovereign houses who married and fought one another for centuries to gain and keep territory and power.

The early Counts of Aragon started to build a power base in the opening decade of the 9th century but their antecedents and precise details are sketchy. It is thought that the dynasty began when Frankish nobles from France migrated to what is now northern Spain.

In 926 the family married into the House of Navarre and the Duchy continued until the reign of Sancho III

The Spanish coat of arms

or The Great when the dukes were transformed into kings – what historians now call the 'Kingdom of Aragon and Navarre'.

In the mid-12th century, Petronila of Aragon married the Count of Barcelona, Ramon Berenguer, creating the dynastic 'House of Barcelona'. During his reign (1213–76), Jaume I conquered Ibiza and Mallorca in c.1228, and Valencia in 1238; his successor, Pedro III, added Sicily. It was Alfonso III who brought Menorca into the fold. The Barcelona line died out with Martin I in 1410 and it was a couple of years before the Trastamara dynasty took the vacant throne.

The dynastic line was solidified in the person of Fernando II (1479–1516) whose reign was undisputed. His marriage to Isabel of Castile is considered by historians to have been a pivotal point in the history of greater Spain – the point when the houses stopped fighting with each other and started working on a wider consensus.

However, the marriage didn't result in a merger of these two royal 'corporations'; it was in many ways an accord rather than a contract, and the two monarchs had quite different priorities. For Fernando, the preservation of his Mediterranean kingdom, including Menorca (but also Sicily and Sardinia), took precedence,

while Isabel was keen to push the Moors from the Iberian peninsula and replace Islam with Christianity. She also funded a little trip by one Christopher Columbus that changed the course of history.

This dynastic alliance of Aragon and Castile thrust the family into the big time as the line quickly produced Carlos I of Spain, better known as Charles V, Holy Roman Emperor (also of the House of Austria). Throughout the 1500s and 1600s, a series of Habsburg (Aragonese) rulers held sway over the area, but in 1700 Carlos II died without heirs.

The power vacuum that followed resulted in the Spanish War of Succession. In 1714, the accession of Archduke Charles of Austria and the consolidation of power in the entity of Spain brought the Catalan–Aragonese confederation to an end.

HOW ARAGON WORKED

The Kingdom of Aragon on mainland Spain was never a true sovereignty. The territory consisted of a series of independent provinces each ruled by a *Cortes* who worked in close consensus with the current ruler. This was much more a mercantile than a territorial or ideological empire, thriving in trade from port cities such as Barcelona. Unfortunately, as time went on, they came under pressure from competitors, including the very successful Genoese, and friction in the eastern Mediterranean took up a lot of their attention.

Politics

Menorca is one of four populated Balearic Islands, which are territorially part of the Spanish nation. The country has had a complicated political history, and today Spain is the most devolved state in Europe, with 17 autonomous regions and 2 autonomous cities. Menorca forms part of the Comunidad Autónoma de las Islas Baleares (Autonomous Region of the Balearic Islands), with a capital at Palma on the largest island, Mallorca. It has its own Consell Insular *(Island Council).*

Historical background

Strong regional identities have deep historic roots in the Spanish peninsula. In the beginning of the 16th century, this country had been a mass of constantly fighting fiefdoms with each rising and falling in influence.

Even after Carlos I (better known as Charles V of Austria) was crowned King of Spain in 1516, some Spanish regions were still given specialist privileges, including Catalunya, and the seemingly unified monarchy was a mass of tensions between the various regional and bloodline factions. As late as 1931, when the government was overthrown and the Second Republic was declared, these were still in play. Catalunya declared itself independent and the Basques and Galicia were on the road to do the same when civil war broke out in 1936; the ensuing bloodbath resulted in the establishment of a military dictatorship headed by General Franco.

Franco suppressed any political debate, ruthlessly suppressing regionalism, but when Spain entered a new era after his death in 1975 it was vitally important to manage these tensions to avoid total meltdown such as that which followed Tito's death in Yugoslavia. The politicians managed this pretty well by recognising and accommodating the differences. In the summer of 1977, a Minister for the Regions was appointed to assess the future. True federalism was ruled out, but during a two-year consultation period an agreement was reached between the various parties to form an autonomous assembly for regions whose populations demanded it.

Spain's prickly language issue was also tackled and the new constitution states that in addition to Castilian, Spain has three other official languages, Basque, Catalan and Galician, though use of these languages is pretty much limited to their specific geographical regions.

Since Spain joined the precursor of the EU in 1986, this regional approach has been strengthened and supported by a pan-European mandate to preserve minority languages and encourage and defend the cultural diversity in the lands within the Union.

The national institutions

Spain is a parliamentary democracy headed by King Juan Carlos I, who took the throne by popular mandate in November 1975. This position is hereditary but the role has no executive power; the monarch is essentially a national figurehead.

The legislative branch of government, Las Cortes Generales, consists of two chambers. The first is the *senado* or senate consisting of 259 seats. Two hundred and eight of these are directly elected and 51 are appointed by the assemblies of the autonomous regions.

The Congress of Deputies is a 350-seat chamber whose members are appointed according to candidate lists under a proportional representation system. Each party is awarded a number of seats corresponding to their percentage of popular vote.

What's happening now

Spain's current government was first elected in April 2004, and went on to win a separate term in 2008; the party is led by the left-wing Socialist Prime Minister José Luis Rodriguez Zapatero. However, the usually more conservative Menorcans stayed true to form and voted for the then incumbent centre-right government led by José María Aznar. The Menorcan Consell Insular (Island Council) has a Conservative majority in the form of the Partido Popular.

The autonomous regions

The islands of the Balearics form one of the 17 autonomous regions of Spain. The rights of the autonomous regions are guaranteed by the constitution. The basic principle of autonomy is that the state recognises and guarantees the right of self-rule in the regions, provided they recognise the sovereignty of the greater Spanish nation.

The specific responsibilities of the governments of the various autonomous

Politics

The Menorcan and Spanish flags

regions vary slightly but include the following:

- Agriculture and forestry
- Commercial fishing (within territorial waters)
- Environmental protection
- Health and hygiene
- Housing
- Local cultural affairs
- Mineral and thermal waters
- Museums and libraries
- Non-commercial ports and airports
- Public works
- Preservation of monuments and historic buildings
- Railways, canals and roads
- Social assistance
- Tourism
- Town planning

The regional assemblies

The regional assemblies consist of a single chamber whose members or *diputados* are elected according to the national system of proportional representation. This system guarantees that all the political demands in communities are represented in the assembly. The *diputados* usually hold office for a period of four years. *Diputados* cannot sit in the national assembly but they do elect the senators who represent the community in the national Senate. Laws passed by regional assemblies are called territorial laws and are equal to, or have priority over, state laws in areas where the local legislature has jurisdiction.

The president

The regional president is the highest representative as well as the symbolic head of the autonomous region and represents the state.

He or she is responsible for the execution of national policy at the regional level and for duties as decided by each individual region, so the job varies from region to region.

Regional executive

The president and a team of ministers form the regional executive. The ministers are chosen from the *diputados* of the assembly and are responsible to them for all duties and decisions.

The judiciary

Each autonomous region has a Tribunal Superior de Justicia, a judicial body that deals with disputes involving regional law. It is also the highest judicial court within the territory; however, it does not supersede the Supreme Court of Justice in Madrid in any matter.

Green politics in action

In a radical and controversial decision in 2003, the autonomous region of the Balearics voted to introduce a tourist tax on each arriving passenger (around €4 per person), which would be funnelled directly into environmentally friendly projects. The tax was unpopular with hoteliers and the big holiday companies, and bookings for the summer of 2004 dropped by over 10 per cent, although surveys did not find a correlation between the levy and the drop in demand. In 2004 the government announced that it was scrapping the tax. A subsequent idea to impose a tax on customers travelling to the island on budget airlines, such as easyJet, from 2008 was similarly scrapped. This was despite the apparently sound motivation for the tax, the idea being to offset the carbon footprint caused by mass tourism to the island.

Looking up at the old town of Maó from Costa de Ses Voltes

Culture

Menorca has mostly been on the fringes of any empire it has been a part of, and its contribution to the arts has not been on a grand scale. Instead, it has concentrated on cultivating its own home-grown 'arts', usually folkloric celebrations enjoyed by the population at fiestas and other holidays. Today, however, there is a lively cultural life and the island has one or two surprises up its sleeve.

Theatre and opera

You will find a surprisingly varied classical arts programme, concentrated in the two main towns of Maó and Ciutadella.

The **Teatre Principal** in Maó, built at the end of the 18th century, is Spain's oldest opera house and the island's premier cultural venue (*Costa d'en Deià 40, Maó; tel: 971 35 56 03; www.teatremao.com*). It is home to the Fundació de Teatre Principal, an organisation that promotes the arts throughout Menorca and offers programmes of classical and modern performances in the elegant neoclassical interior. At the time of writing, this theatre was closed and up for sale. It faces an uncertain future.

The **Teatre des Born** on Plaça d'es Born in Ciutadella is the major cultural venue in western Menorca (*Plaça d'es Born; Ciutadella town hall; tel: 971 38 10 50*). It hosts plays, opera and other live music throughout the year. At the time of writing, it was closed, but due

to reopen later in 2011 after major renovations. On the outskirts of Ciutadella, the **Pedreres de s'Hostal** (the old quarry, *see pp125–6*) has been imaginatively turned into an open-air venue and is gaining a reputation for its great acoustics (*Camí Vell; 1km/²/₃ mile east of town; tel: 971 48 15 78*).

Famous voices

The island's most famous living son is Joan Pons Álvarez, born in Ciutadella in 1946 and now one of the world's foremost operatic baritones. Pons made his debut at Milan's La Scala in 1980 and has also performed at London's Covent Garden and the Metropolitan Opera House in New York. He continues to perform occasionally on his home island, but tickets sell out instantly so you will be lucky to catch a performance.

Opera singer Lluis Sintes, born in Maó, has followed in Pons' footsteps by performing internationally. Simon Orfila, another baritone from the island, completes the triumvirate.

Art

The island has a strong commitment to art, and several cultural centres host exhibitions by local and international artists. English watercolourist Graham Byfield has set up shop in Es Migjorn Gran (*see pp107–8*) and Galleria Arantza and Cia Art sell contemporary Menorcan artwork in Alaior (*see pp101–2*).

Two notable local luminaries are Jose Torrent and Pere Daura I Garcia.

Jose Torrent

Jose Torrent was born in Ciutadella in 1904. Throughout his life he travelled the island, painting the landscapes in strong vivid colours; he became known to the locals as the 'Menorcan Van Gogh'. Torrent died in 1990 and his old

Square by the cathedral in Ciutadella

home in the town has been converted into a museum displaying over 100 original works that span his long career, plus many personal artefacts.
Museu Pintor-Torrent, Ciutadella. Carrer Sant Rafael 11. Tel: 971 38 04 82. Open: Jun–Oct daily 11am–1pm & 7.30–9.30pm; Nov–May Fri–Sat 5–9pm.

Pere Daura I Garcia

Born in Ciutadella while his family was on a trip away from their native Barcelona, Daura trained in Barcelona, where he was taught by Picasso's father. In 1914 he ventured to Paris where he became entranced by Fauvism.

In 1928 he married American artist Louise Blair and on their honeymoon they fell in love with a medieval mansion in St-Cirq Lapopie in France. In the late 1920s Daura toyed with Abstract art as a founder of the Cercle se Cercle group with close ties to Kandinsky, Léger and Mondrian. He returned to Spain to fight for the Republicans in the Civil War but later, in 1943, settled permanently in the US, spending his summers in France. He died in 1976.

An exhibition of Daura's paintings is on permanent display at the Museu Diocesà de Menorca in Ciutadella (*see p125*).

Traditional music and dance

Although there are clubs dotted around the island such as the Casino jazz club in Sant Climent and the famous Cova d'en Xoroi hip hop, trance and house club in Cala'n Porter (*see p102*), local, traditional music holds the hearts of Menorcans. Traditional dance accompanied by traditional music has increased in popularity since the fall of the Franco regime, and many dance troupes across the island perform traditional displays.

Groups like the Arrels de Sant Joan from Ciutadella and Castell de Sant Filipe from Es Castell perform regularly around the island, usually at weekends. Every year the folk group Es Rebost organises the **Ballades a sa Plaça**, a programme of performances held at the Claustre del Carme (*see p39*) in Maó (*Jun–Sept Thur 8.30pm; free admission*). These offer the perfect opportunity to get to know traditional Menorcan music, dances (*see below*) and dresses, besides other Spanish dances like the *fandango* and *bolero*.

The *jota* is the most traditional of the Catalan dances, a performance by two people, accompanied in medieval times by a song. It was originally performed at wakes and funeral meetings to celebrate the dead but it is now a part of every traditional display. The *Jota de Aragon* is famous throughout Spain.

A BRITISH TOUCH

Es Castell (the old British Georgetown) still takes pride in its Scottish dances, where the performers wear kilts like the old Scottish regimental soldiers who used to be based here. However, the dancers perform to the sounds of the very Balearic *flabiol* and *tamborí*.

In the Balearics, the *jota* spawned the *mateixa*. This is also performed by two dancers, but after each set of movements, one of the dancers is replaced by a fresh performer so that it is almost like a dance 'round'.

The *copeo* has a faster tempo and is a group dance for several couples. Tradition links it to celebrations, performed when a pig was slaughtered and roasted.

Cossiers are thought to be the oldest dances of the Balearics, and may well be an archaic vestige of complex ceremonies used by an old cult in the worship of agricultural deities because they are related to planting and harvest times. The dancers are men (always six in number) dressed as women, and they wear skirts and wide-brimmed hats decorated with flowers, ribbons and bells. They carry branches of basil and a handkerchief. With them is saintly *Dama de Cossiers* (Lady of the Cossiers) and a devil, representing a confrontation between good and evil.

Musical instruments

Menorcan dances have simple traditional musical accompaniment – the *flabiol*, a small wooden flute with five finger holes that are played with the left hand, and the *tamborí*, a small side drum played with the right hand. The guitar came later in the island's history but is now an integral element of the greater 'Spanish' musical experience.

Motor scooters parked in Carrer d'Isabel II, Maó

Architectural styles

The colonial stewardship of Menorca over the years brought many architectural styles to the island. This is a quick guide to the post-ancient Roman architectural styles found here.

Early Christian/Byzantine

Named after Byzantium (or Constantinople), the capital of the Christian world in the late first millennium, this religious style was erected on a rectangular ground plan with a simple open structure and an entrance from the west. The floor plans can be seen at the basilicas at des Fornàs de Torelló (*see pp68–9*) and Son Bou (*see pp112–13*).

Moorish

The Moors introduced the narrow arch into architecture; later, the style became recognisable by its pointed peak. Although many buildings were erected during their custody of Menorca, because of the animosity of the local people, the only Islamic architectural element left on the island is the tower of Ciutadella cathedral.

Casa Mir from the early 20th century

Gothic

The Gothic style was a development of the Romanesque and its main feature is the pointed arch, which became extremely fine as the style developed. In churches and cathedrals, the western façade was the most impressive exterior feature, and these became more and more ornate over time. The south portal of the cathedral at Ciutadella is typical of the style.

Renaissance

The Renaissance or 'rebirth' revolutionised the arts in the 14th–16th centuries. The architectural style harked back to the Roman classics, including the four styles of columns and the arch. However, Menorca has few fine Renaissance buildings, as many were destroyed in the later Ottoman raids. Seek out Ermita de Sant Llorenc south of Arenal d'en Castell (*see p86*).

Baroque

The Baroque style was fashionable from the late-16th to mid-18th centuries, and is characterised by ornate decoration with the aid of columns, domes, pilasters and entablature. In Spain, a highly ornate form of Baroque called Churrigueresque, after architect José Benito de Churriguera, became popular. This Churrigueresque style can be viewed on the façade of the Església del Roser (*see p124*) in Ciutadella.

Neoclassical

A backlash against Baroque in the late 18th century brought the purer lines now called the neoclassical style. Its main characteristics are clean and uncluttered lines based on the mathematical formulae used by the ancient Greeks. The British military and naval complexes at Es Castell (*see pp52–4*) and at the naval base (*see p63*) are good examples.

Art Nouveau and Art Deco

The two movements that kick-started the 20th century often used glass and iron in their designs. Art Nouveau was characterised by curved lines, while Art Deco moved on to a modern interpretation of classical straight lines. Casa Mir (*see p46*) and the Fish Market (*see p48*), both in Maó, are two contrasting early 20th-century buildings.

Domestic architecture

Llocs are traditional Menorcan farm complexes. These buildings are erected around a courtyard with a south-facing house and *porxada* – a large vaulted porch where the family live for much of the summer. There are barns and stables on the north side to protect the house against the prevailing *tramuntana* wind.

Festivals and events

You will find a packed programme of cultural events throughout the year in Menorca. Religious festivals are favoured, with Christmas, Carnival, Easter and Assumption Day being the most important. Parades are held across the island on these occasions, with Easter being the time for more reverent processions. Sacred statues or paintings are solemnly paraded through the streets before the party begins.

In addition to this, every settlement has a *festa* (Castilian – *fiesta*) or feast day, celebrating the local patron saint. Further gatherings take place around harvest time when nature's bounty is celebrated. Menorca also holds several sporting events, though none that breaks on to the international stage.

The following list only scratches the surface of events, so consult the tourist office to find out about what is happening during your stay on the island. *See pp154–5 and 158–9 for more details.*

January
Diada de Sant Antoni (St Anthony's Day) has island-wide festivities and bonfires to honour the patron saint of Menorca. (17th)
Processo dels Tres Tocs, when Ciutadella celebrates the retaking of the island by Alfonso III in 1287. (17th)

March/April
Semana Santa (Holy Week) parades.

May
Festa de la Verge del Toro (*see pp110–11*) with a Mass on Monte Toro and festivities in Es Mercadal. (8th)
Menorca International Jazz Festival There are performances all around the island. (all month)

June
Festa de Sant Joan (St John), the festival highlight of the year in Ciutadella (*see p129*). (23rd–24th)
The **Menorcan-Sant Joan Sailing Regatta** in the port of Maó. (late June)

July
Ciutadella remembers the fateful attack of the Turks in 1558 (*see p12*), which started the 'year of misfortune'. (9th)
St Martí celebrations at Es Mercadal; Ciutadella holds the marine parade of Verge del Carme. (mid-month)
Procession of the Virgin of Carme in the port at Maó. (16th)
Es Castell celebrates the **Festa de Sant Jaume** (St James). (24th–26th)

Sant Antoni (St Anthony) celebrations at Fornells. (20th–22nd)

Sant Cristòfol (St Christopher) celebrations in Es Migjorn Gran. (28th–30th)

The **Festival de Musica d'Estiu** (*see p154*) classical concert season in Ciutadella. (throughout July & August)

The **Maó International Music Festival** (*see p154*) with classical concerts at the Església de Santa Maria and occasionally other venues. (throughout mid-July–mid-September)

Primavera Cultural and **Estiu à Ferreries** traditional music and dance at Ferreries. (throughout July–September)

Colourful festival decorations in Maó

CALENDAR OF LOCAL RELIGIOUS FESTIVALS

Ciutadella	Sant Joan 23–24 June
Es Mercadel	Sant Martí 13–15 July
Es Castell	Sant Jaume 24–26 July
Fornells	Sant Antoni 20–22 July
Es Migjorn Gran	Sant Cristòfol 28–30 July
Alaior	Sant Llorenç 11–13 August
Sant Climent	Sant Climent 18–20 August
Ferreries	Sant Bartomeu 23–25 August
Sant Lluís	Sant Lluís 24–26 August
Maó	La Verge de Gràcia 7–9 Sept

August

Festa de Sant Llorenç (St Lawrence) with jousting in Alaior. (11th–13th)

Copa del Rey de Barcos de Época (*see p158*), a boat regatta with craft either vintage (pre-1949) or classic (1950–75), racing off Maó and mooring at the port by night. (late in the month)

Festa de Sant Climent (St Clement) in the town of the same name. (18th–20th)

Festa de Sant Bartomeu (St Bartholomew) at Ferreries. (23rd–25th)

September

La Verge de Gràcia celebrations at Maó. (7th–9th)

Festival of St Nicholas at the summit of Monte Toro. (10th)

October

Fun half-marathon (*see p158*) around the streets of Ciutadella. (1st)

Vuelta Cicloturistica, an amateur cycling tour (*see p160*) of the island. (third/fourth week)

Impressions

Sitting in the Mediterranean Sea just east of Spain, Menorca is the easternmost of 11 islands and islets that make up the Balearic Islands. Apart from Menorca, only three other islands are populated – Mallorca, Ibiza and Formentera – and each one offers a different landscape and character. As compared to the 'party' islands of Ibiza and Mallorca, Menorca could be considered the island for family fun and the 'great outdoors'.

When to go

Summer

Glorious blue skies, daytime temperatures in the upper 20s°C (80s°F), several hours of guaranteed sunshine and long warm evenings draw thousands of visitors in the summer. Menorca is the epitome of the Mediterranean holiday destination in this season, with the beaches coming into their own, offering excellent swimming, snorkelling and diving opportunities and great boat trips if you don't want to get wet.

Of course, the downside of the peak season (late June–mid-Sept) is the sheer numbers of visitors putting pressure on the infrastructure. Roads, restaurants, marinas and hotels are chock-a-block, and it may be a little too hot for any strenuous activity like hiking and cycling.

Autumn

The crowds depart by the end of September, and churches and museums, plus the narrow alleys of Maó and Ciutadella, become easier to explore. You will be able to find seats in the fashionable cafés once again and the roads are less congested. Temperatures are moderate in this season and great for outdoor sports and activities, and the sun's warm glow is better for photographers than the harsh high summer light. For birdwatchers, autumn is when the migratory birds stop off on their long journey south, making it an ideal time to visit.

The downside of a late visit is that the weather becomes less dependable with more chances of cloud cover and the odd spectacular thunderstorm. The evenings are cooler, so alfresco dinners might be off the menu.

Winter

By now the tourist crowds have long departed and many resorts seem to be completely closed; however, the winter season does have its compensations. Temperatures are warmer than in northern Europe, offering good conditions for hiking and cycling. You will also find a genuinely Catalan atmosphere around the island with the locals getting on with life. Just watch out for the biting *tramuntana*, the wind that really chills the air in the northern parts of the island.

Spring
Temperatures start rising again, as do the hours of sunlight. The birds return – heading north this time – and leaves on trees and budding crops look ahead to another fertile year. The canopies and umbrellas of the phalanx of waterside cafés and restaurants open like flowers, signalling that it's time for business.

The *tramuntana* warms a touch but can still inflict a nasty sting when the temperature occasionally drops.

In and out of season
Historically, the regular charter packages from the UK and other parts of northern Europe tended to fly to Menorca from early May to the end of October, and many hotels closed out of this 'season', making accommodation more difficult to come by. With the advent of cheaper budget flights, this is changing, with the major hotels staying open for longer. However, many resort facilities will still close down in the winter months. If new taxes are ever introduced on budget flights (*see p19*) this again might have a bearing on the length of Menorca's tourist 'season'.

What to wear
Layering is the byword here. In summer, light cotton or breathable

Terraced sunbathing areas at Cala'n Brut

clothing is advisable for sightseeing. Take a long-sleeved top to avoid your arms and shoulders getting sunburnt, but the weather is reliable, so you shouldn't need warm clothing. Swimsuits are not considered suitable attire for the towns and should be confined to the beaches – where topless bathing is perfectly acceptable.

Spring and autumn are warm, so carry light cotton outfits, but also pack a couple of warm layers (a fleece is ideal) especially for the evenings. The island can witness spectacular storms so a weatherproof jacket might be useful.

In the winter months, warm and waterproof clothing is advisable, although it certainly isn't unusual to be able to wear T-shirts during the day in December or January. The evenings, however, will be chilly.

Whatever time of year you visit, it is wise to take clothing that will cover the thighs and shoulders if you intend to visit churches and *ermitas*. These are spiritual places to those who worship here and you'll be considered disrespectful if you visit scantily dressed.

What to see and do

Without a doubt, the beaches are the primary draw of the island. The main resorts all have beautiful stretches and, although most get crowded in August, it is easy to head out along the coast and find an equally, if not more, beautiful and less populated stretch of sand where you can lay out your towel and bronze to your heart's content.

Menorca is rich in prehistoric remains and you may want to visit at least one of the dozens of Talayotic sites scattered across the island. If your interest is whetted you could fill a week or two and visit them all.

The two major settlements, Maó and Ciutadella – called cities though in size little more than large towns – are unmissable for their architecture and atmosphere. Both have picturesque ports with a jaunty nautical air, and great bars and shops.

Between days of sightseeing you can take to the water to windsurf or kayak or sail, head under the water with snorkel or scuba, get out on the country lanes on foot, bicycle or on horse, and grab a pair of binoculars to see the spectacular wildlife.

Menorca has some excellent and inexpensive restaurants where you can relax in the evenings over a long, satisfying dinner.

Getting around

The bus services in Menorca are excellent for touring the main towns, with several Maó-to-Ciutadella connections every day travelling through Alaior, Es Mercadal and Ferreries. There are also direct bus services to the capital from Punta Prima and the resorts of the southeast, and also from Maó to Es Grau and Fornells in the northeast and north respectively. Ciutadella is well linked to its surrounding resorts with regular services to Cala'n Forcat and Cala'n

Bosch. In the major resorts you will find private companies who offer day tours by bus to the main attractions, often with a guide and lunch included.

Driving in Menorca

To explore the remote beaches and the dozens of ancient sites dotted around the island, you really need to rent a car, even if only for a couple of days. A rental car puts you in charge of your own timetable and this is a relatively easy place to drive in, with narrow lanes keeping speeds down, and no dual carriageways or fast roads to worry about. Menorcans are

used to thousands of rental cars on their roads every summer, and are generally patient and courteous towards visitors. Beware of the over-zealous police, who seem to spend most of their time hiding around corners in the road waiting to nab speeding cars.

Like the rest of Spain, Menorca drives on the right. Speed limits (*see p180*) are rigidly adhered to. Seat belts must be worn at all times. If you break down, put on the reflective jacket before getting out of the car on the road and immediately deploy the warning triangle. Check that jacket and

Sunday lunchtime in Ferreries

triangle are both in your hire car before departure. There are several petrol stations around Maó and Ciutadella, and along the main road between the two, but there are few on the rest of the island so keep the tank topped up.

Cultural traits

You are bound to find a few unusual and noteworthy differences between your homeland and Menorca. The following thoughts are a truly non-scientific approach to the idiosyncrasies of the island. They are in no particular order but simply offer a flavour of the national mindset.

Catalan and Castilian

Since Catalan has replaced Castilian as the official language of the island (*see pp34–5*), you will notice names being changed and street signs duplicated so that Castilian Mahón becomes Catalan Maó, Alayor becomes Alaior and so on. Some of these changes take time, so don't be surprised to find different spellings for town and street names on maps and other tourist literature. In this book we have used the most common Catalan spellings unless the Castilian name is still used.

Siesta time

One factor that you must take into account when planning your sightseeing is siesta time. Because it is so hot in the summer it has become the tradition for everything to close in the afternoon when everyone rests or has a short nap, and for shops, museums, bars and restaurants to reopen as the air cools. Siesta time is usually from around 1pm until 4pm or 5pm. You will find that the major settlements away from the coast turn into ghost towns between these hours. However, you won't find the same in the holiday resorts where shops and restaurants remain open throughout the day.

How late?

Menorcans are fresh and raring to go in the evenings. They rarely eat before 9pm and often wait until later at weekends or on holidays. Children are still playing happily as midnight approaches and the streets are buzzing into the early hours of the morning, although there is never evidence of the

Statue of the Virgin Mary in a shrine

drunken raucous behaviour found after a night out in northern Europe. If you want your children to stay up late as well, remember to let them have a sleep in the afternoon.

The *paseo*

The evening stroll is a Spanish institution. This is the time when neighbours chat, recent parents parade their babies, grandparents bill and coo, and courting couples only have eyes for each other. Weekend evenings see everyone dressed in their finest clothes. For prime people-watching, try the port at Ciutadella on a Saturday night.

Ice cream

An ice cream is compulsory during the evening *paseo* and not just for children. Delicious sorbets and delicate fruit flavours entice adults too! You'll find shops and stalls offering dozens of flavours in all of the major towns as well as in the tourist spots on the coast.

An ice cream for the *paseo* in Ciutadella

Catalan v. Castilian

To new arrivals in Menorca, the Catalan v. Castilian debate can seem confusing and irrelevant, but this issue cuts to the very heart of the Menorcan identity.

Both languages are classed as Iberian Romance languages, also known as 'New Latin', and they travelled south in the wake of the Reconquista (the pushing back of Moorish control south through the Iberian peninsula, *see p11*).

At that time, different feudal power bases controlled different geographical areas – the rulers of Castile in central Spain spoke Castilian, while Catalan was spoken by the Aragonese in Catalunya in northeast Spain, which also held sway over the Balearics in the wake of the Moorish retreat in the 13th century.

These two powerful dynasties were in constant battle with each other in the intervening centuries, but eventually, after many inter-dynastic marriages, they reached an accord with the marriage of Fernando of Aragon and Isabel of Castile in 1469.

* **NAVEGUI POC A POC PER DINS DE LA CALA**

* *NAVEGA DESPACIO POR LA CALA*

Most signboards are dual-language, with instructions in Catalan and Castilian

The Aragonese were preoccupied with their Italian and Mediterranean territories and Castilian became the majority language across mainland Spain, although Catalan was used within its traditional geographical boundaries. The Castilian language was spread across the New World with the establishment of the Spanish colonies and became the lead dialect as administration developed.

This may not have mattered much when most Menorcans did not have much to do with life in Madrid or even on the mainland, but when Franco won the Civil War in 1939 he had a clear vision of what he wanted his Spain to be. In addition to ruthlessly stamping out any political opposition or dissent, he sought to quash many of the regional peculiarities of what was still a very diverse society, including the Catalan language.

Catalan printing presses were destroyed and newspapers closed down, and the teaching of the language in schools was banned. Although many Menorcans continued to learn to speak Catalan at home, fewer learnt to write it, and it wasn't until after Franco's death in 1975 that things started to change. After Spain joined the precursor of the EU in 1986, Catalan rose like a phoenix from the ashes of the dictatorship, nurtured by the European pledge to preserve regional or minority languages.

Today, Catalan is the official language of Catalunya, Valencia and the Balearics, and it is the primary language in schools and for all official institutions on Menorca. There are several daily newspapers printed in Catalan, including *El Día del Mundo de Baleares and Ultima Hora*; Televisio Catalunya broadcasts across the region in Catalan and there is a 24-hour news channel.

Franco's legacy is that most Menorcans of native stock (as opposed to recent arrivals from mainland Spain) now speak both Catalan and Castilian, and you will have no trouble making yourself understood in Castilian, nor will you come across any animosity if you communicate in Castilian. However, if you learn a few phrases in Catalan, the already warm welcome will be just a little warmer and the wide smile just a little wider.

QUICK FACTS

Catalan: spoken by 7.5 million people in Andorra, Catalunya, Murcia, Valencia and the Balearic Islands in Spain; also Roussillon in France and Alghero on Sardinia. Understood by a total of 12 million people.
Castilian: spoken by 330 million people in Spain and South and Central America, with large populations of speakers in the USA. Understood by 417 million people.

Maó

Capital of the island since the 18th century, Maó is as bustling as Menorca gets but it is also a very approachable, attractive and relaxed city where you don't feel overwhelmed by urbanisation.

Most visitors come overland from the resorts on the south and west coasts of the island through the little jumble of modern suburbs, but that was never the city's *raison d'être*. It thrived on its relationship with the sea and its sheltered position close to the head of the inlet, and you get the best feel of

Maó City

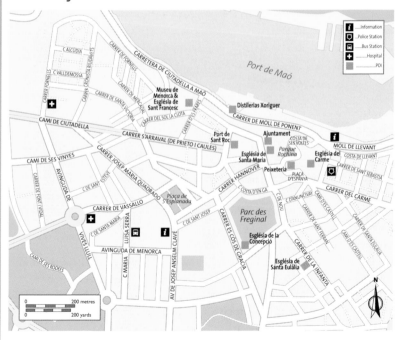

the old heartbeat by starting your tour at Maó port. From the waterside the buildings of the old town seem to grow out of the rock, presenting a sheer face of sandstone and stucco hanging above the port and harbour below.

Once atop the cliffs you will find a compact old town of fine 18th- and 19th-century mansions, which are held together by a web of narrow lanes and alleyways interspersed with tiny communal squares. Grand old entranceways lead into three-storeyed houses whose windows are guarded with fretted ironwork and shutters; the historical and religious attractions are firmly planted in the heart of this comfortable domesticity.

Maó became capital of Menorca only during the 18th century, and even then the religious hierarchy refused to decamp from their archdiocese at Ciutadella (*see pp121–8*). Nevertheless, the British went ahead and shifted the focus of the island to the east in 1722, away from its siblings Mallorca and Ibiza. Today, although the city was founded by the Royal Navy and there are still a few small British touches, Maó is very much a Catalan Spanish town. There has been a quiet confidence about the place since the demise of the Franco regime, the resurrection of the Catalan language and the decentralisation of power from Madrid to the Balearics.

The city has easily enough attractions to fill a day. The Museu de Menorca is a must-visit attraction to help add a human story to the numerous ancient sites you will visit during your stay. But perhaps it is the atmosphere in the capital's streets that makes it most worth a visit – especially in the early evening when the entire population takes to the streets to stroll, socialise and romance. There is certainly a Latin magic about the place that lasts late into the evening.

Ajuntament (Town Hall)

The Town Hall was built in 1613 on the site of a medieval fortress but was given a smart new French Baroque overcoat in 1789 by architect Francisco Fernàndez de Angelo. The small clock was an afterthought added by Governor Kane (*see pp66–7*). It has a splendid façade replete with wrought-iron balconies and pompous pediments but it is difficult to admire the exterior because it sits on a corner of Plaça de Sa Constitució, plagued by passing cars and pedestrians. The building really deserves a better location.

The interior decoration is sumptuous, particularly the paintings and plasterwork in the Noble Hall and the Gallery of the Illustrious Menorcans. There is also a portrait of British King George III who ruled during much of his country's occupation of the island.

The buildings to the left of the Town Hall are also worth a look for their eclectic Modernist architecture.
Plaça de Sa Constitució. Open: to the public daily 8am–2pm.

Shopping on Carrer Hannover in Maó

Carrer Hannover

A continuation of the main shopping street that runs from Plaça de s'Esplanada to Plaça de Sa Constitució, Carrer Hannover is named after the Royal House of Hanover, which ruled Britain in the 18th century (the spelling difference was originally accidental but has become official). Although Maó offers many examples of domestic architecture, this short section of the street is one of the most complete vistas in the city – an uninterrupted run of several buildings characterised by English details such as sash and bowed windows, the latter known in Spanish as *boinders*.

Costa de Ses Voltes and Parque Rochina

This winding lane flanked by a small manicured park and a grand staircase for pedestrians was, until the mid-20th century, a wide ramp used to move cargo up to town from the port. Today there is usually lots of parking along the winding road, and the gardens are a place for children to play, lovers to meet and old folks to sit and watch the world go by.

At either side of the base of the Costa you can view the remains of the old city walls that once protected Maó. The medieval and later Renaissance structures now form the foundations of more modern buildings, which seem to grow out of the cliffs lining the port.

Distilerias Xoriguer (Xoriguer Distillery)

The leading manufacturer of the distinctive Menorcan gin (*see pp172–3*), Xoriguer is a family-owned company that launched the brand on the UK market in 2005. Xoriguer is still housed in one of the old warehouses down on the port side and you can see the distillery vats and old copper stills working their magic.

Xoriguer allow you to sample all their products before you buy, and there is ample information in English about the ingredients in each – although not the exact quantities, as the recipes are a guarded secret. *Distilerias Xoriguer. Carrer de Moll de Ponent 91. Tel: 971 36 21 97.*

www.xoriguer.es. Open: Jun–Sept
Mon–Fri 8am–7pm, Sat 9am–1pm;
Oct–May Mon–Fri 9am–1pm & 4–7pm.

Església del Carme
(Carmelite Church)

The Carmelite order gained permission
from the British to build a church and
convent, the Claustre del Carme, and
the authorities approved a site high
above the harbour, which stood outside
the city walls at the time. The work was
started in 1750 but coincided with a
turbulent few decades in the island
between the British, French and
Spanish, and the complex was not
completed until 1820. The huge façade
almost imitates Port St Roc (*see pp46 &*
47) with its two towers. It is devoid of
embellishment save an extended arch
around the doorway. This is the largest
church in Maó but one of its least
decorated.

The cloisters here were almost
immediately deconsecrated when the
civil authorities grabbed church
property across Spain, and they have
been used for a number of civic
purposes since 1835, including
courtrooms and a prison. Today they
serve as the city's arcaded food market,
which also has lots of stalls selling
jewellery and leather goods to visitors –
well worth exploring in the morning.

The cloisters also play host to the
Museu Hernández Mora (Hernández
Mora Museum). This museum is
dedicated to the collections of Joan
Hernández Mora, who was a Victorian-
era scientist, an art professor,
archaeologist, archivist, artist and
historian. His collection dates from
1949 and comprises numerous works
of art, furniture and household
artefacts from the 18th to the 20th
centuries, a cartography collection
and a library of works by Menorcan
authors. The museum also hosts
temporary art exhibitions.

In front of the cloisters is a small patio
where locals gather for a coffee in noisy
Café Bar Mirador. There are excellent
views down to the harbour from here.
Museu Hernández Mora. Claustre
del Carme 5. Tel: 971 35 05 97.
Open: Mon–Sat 10am–1pm.
Free admission.

Església del Carme entrance

Església de Sant Francesc (Church of St Francis)

Although the cloisters of the Franciscan monastery complex now house the Museum of Menorca (see pp42–5), the adjoining church is still open for worship. Built on the foundations of an earlier Gothic church, the building of the present church was begun in 1719, and it was expanded throughout the century. The façade was not added until the 1800s.

The interior displays a single nave – as with the other major churches in the city. The major decorative elements, including paintings in the presbytery, are also 19th century. The mock-Baroque *retablo* (painting or framed image) above the main altar was added in 1945. The Chapel of the Immaculate Conception is probably the finest part of the church. Completed in 1752, the octagonal structure topped by an impressive cupola is linked to the main nave by a grand entrance portal. The decoration is extremely rich, with a never-ending stream of carved vines and acanthus leaves in Churrigueresque style, attributed to artist Francesc Herrara. *Avinguda Doctor Guàrdia. Open: daily 10am–noon & 5–7pm (closed Thur pm).*

Església de Santa Maria (St Mary's Church)

The first church of Santa Maria, patron saint of Maó, was erected by Alfonso III when he claimed the island in 1287. The church was totally rebuilt on the same ground plan in the 18th century in simple neo-Gothic style, so large that the interior is almost hangar-like. However, the main altar and side chapels are Baroque, their high drama a contrast to the lines of the basic architecture.

The other major attraction of the interior is the vast organ built by master organ builders Otter and Kirburz and the central feature of many of Maó's music festivals. Its shape echoes that of the altar with towering columns topped by triumphant statues, though the monotone gold/bronze colour lends an air of gravitas. *Plaça de Sa Constitució. Open: daily 7.30am–1pm & 6–8.30pm. Organ recitals between Apr and Oct Mon–Sat at 11.30am.*

ALFONSO III

Though Jaume I took Menorca from the Moors for the house of Aragon, he did not expel them from the island and left its administration in the hands of a Muslim *reis* or governor. It was not until 1287 that Islam was totally swept away, by Alfonso III, grandson of Jaume, and it is he who is revered by the people of the islands for regaining their independence. There is a statue of Alfonso in Plaça de Constitució (on the north side of Església de Santa Maria). It was presented to the island by General Franco in the 1950s.

Es Port (The Waterfront)

There is a lively atmosphere throughout the summer along the waterfront below the town. Once the heartbeat of the city, the economic

Es Port is a popular dock for yachters

impact of the port has diminished somewhat since the advent of tourism and the building of the airport, but commercial cargo and ferries from the mainland are still a regular feature. The yachting fraternity dock here for the restaurants and bars, and there is some great nightlife too.

Costa de Ses Voltes links the upper town at Plaça d'Espanya (see pp45–6) to the waterfront.

At the base of Ses Voltes you will find a gaily coloured collection of boats offering trips around the harbour. Mediterranean cruise ships dock here – one of their most satisfying ports of call since you can step right out of the ship directly into the town. The main city tourist office is also at the port, facing the main road.

To the west (left from the bottom of Costa de Ses Voltes) you will find the working heart of the port along Moll de Ponent: docks for cruise ships and, as you walk further towards the head of the inlet, ship repair yards and dry docks. You may want to make a trip to the Xoriguer Distillery (see pp38–9) housed in one of the old warehouses on the inland side of the port road.

To the east (right from the bottom of Ses Voltes) is a delightful route along the Moll de Llevant, the main pleasure dock of the city, where you will be accompanied by the sounds of hundreds of halyards jangling in the breeze. On the quayside look out for the life-size bronze statue, *The Maó Mermaid* by Leonardo Lucarni, a symbol of the city and the port. There is a never-ending choice of cafés, bars and restaurants set under the crags where you can sit and watch the action, and in summer the fun goes on until dawn.

Museu de Menorca (Museum of Menorca)

Housed in a section of the monastery complex of St Francis of Assisi, the Museum of Menorca is the island's primary archaeological and historical collection, leading from the very awakening of the ancient lifestyles into the late second millennium.

The building itself demands some attention. Once through the ticket office, the magnificent Baroque cloister was completed just before the religious community was forced to leave in 1835, at the same time as the Carmelite community housed in the Claustre del

The Museum of Menorca

The Maó Mermaid sits on the quayside

Carme complex (*see p39*). The building has had a colourful history: among other purposes, it has operated as a children's home, public library and high school. Architecturally, the fine stonework with its delicate and constrained embellishment, and the balanced form of the tiers of archways and windows, is satisfying to the eye.

Temporary exhibitions are held on the ground floor of the building, while the museum occupies the upper two floors. The galleries are arranged chronologically with captions in English explaining what and where.

The first floor is devoted to the period from prehistory until the Byzantine era. Start off with the

Cut-price flamenco dresses for sale in the market on Plaça de s'Esplanada

pre-Talayotic finds of pre-1500 BC and move into the Talayotic era proper where you will find artefacts of extreme sophistication – including the bronze statue of a bull found at the Torralba d'en Salort (*see pp81 & 115*) that is fundamental to research into the religious beliefs of the Talayotic peoples. There are also interesting pieces from other cultures, including a statue of Imhotep, the Egyptian High Priest, from around 2600 BC, and Punic pottery from mainland Italy. The Roman galleries include finds from a shipwreck off the Cap de Favàritx.

On the second floor, the time line starts with scant remains of the Moors and Aragonese. There are few artefacts from either time because the remaining population destroyed most Islamic buildings in the wake of their withdrawal and many Aragonese remains were lost in the Ottoman raids of the 1530s. The 17th and 18th centuries are well represented through paintings, maps and English china plus some fine Catholic religious statuary rescued from churches across the island. As the Spanish finally took full control of the Balearics, industry arrived on the island, and the later

AND SO TO MARKET

Maó's main tourist market takes place every Tuesday and Saturday morning at Plaça de s'Esplanada, a huge open space that was once a parade ground for the British regiments stationed in the capital. Search among the colourful sarongs and African jewellery for antiques and organic soaps.

MAÓ'S GREEN SPACES

Although the streets of the city centre are narrow and cramped, there are lots of tiny squares lined with palm trees and dotted with pocket-sized grassy areas to relax in. Plaça de s'Esplanada is surrounded by trees and Parc des Freginal is only a few steps away, with enough room for youngsters to let off steam.

galleries document this process. The final gallery displays paintings by 20th-century Menorcan artists, including the 'Group Menorca', a school dedicated to abstract expressionism.

Next door to the museum is Església de Sant Francesc (*see p40*), the church of the original monastery complex. *Museu de Menorca. Avinguda Doctor*

*Guàrdia. Tel: 971 35 09 55.
Open: Apr–Oct Tue–Sat 10am–2pm & 6–8.30pm, Sun 10am–2pm; Nov–Mar Tue–Fri 9.30am–2pm, Sat–Sun 10am–2pm. Closed: Mon.
Admission charge.*

Plaça d'Espanya

For travellers arriving by boat, Plaça d'Espanya is the starting point for exploring the old town, and it is a rather confusing site. Designed in the 20th century during a major reconstruction of the city, it is classed as one of the major squares in the capital, yet it is not really a discernible square since it lies on a sloping piece of land and doesn't have a defined shape. The fish market sits on

A view of Maó and the harbour

the north flank, while the main section of the square that links it to Plaça de Carme and its vast church (*see p39*) is cut by a couple of roads and a very difficult intersection leading down to Costa de Ses Voltes (*see p48*). Near here is the Mercat Claustre del Carme, where former church cloisters have been stylishly converted into a shopping centre and market. The most impressive building in the square sits on the northwestern corner overlooking the port. Casa Mir (not open to the public) was built in the 1920s and, with an elaborate glass façade, is the finest Modernist building on Menorca.

ST ROC

St Roc was a 13th-century French nobleman who became famous for saving towns and villages from the ravages of the plague. Legend dictates that he also saved Maó from infection and a gate in the city wall was dedicated to him. Eventually he contracted the disease himself and wandered into the forest to die, where he was tended by a dog and recovered. In addition to being patron saint of plague sufferers, St Roc apparently also helps people with knee problems and skin rashes.

Peixeteria (Fish Market)

Built on the foundations of an old bastion of the city wall in 1927 to a

A pretty ecclesiastical corner of Maó

Looking over the harbour from Costa de Ses Voltes

design by municipal architect Francesc Femenías, Maó's fish market is an excellent example of Modernist iron-and-glass design still used to this day. You'll find fresh fish and shellfish on ice here, plus live crabs and lobster – the perfect place to shop for dinner if you are self-catering.
Plaça d'Espanya. Open: Mon–Sat 8am–1pm.

Port de St Roc

Incongruously surrounded by a phalanx of narrow streets, Port de St Roc is the only vestige of the old medieval city wall and marked the city's boundary until the 18th century. The two strong towers rise above the rooftops, their slender arrow slits the main base for attack. The narrow entry portal now poses a problem for the

two-way traffic that tries to muscle its way through, but when it was closed every night during medieval times the population would have slept soundly in their beds, secure within the walls. That was until 1535, when Barbarossa swept through the defences and ravaged the city. The gate, along with the rest of the walls, was badly damaged and had to be totally rebuilt. Pretty Plaça del Bastió tucked behind the gate is lined with bars and restaurants and buzzes in the evening.

FOR MORE INFORMATION

The main tourist office in Maó is situated at: *Moll de Llevant 2 (on the waterfront at the bottom of the Costa de Ses Voltes). Tel: 971 35 26 74. www.gocatalunya.com.* The municipal tourist office is at: *Carrer sa Rovellada de Dalt 24. Tel: 971 36 37 90.*

Walk: A tour of Maó

Maó is easy to explore on foot, with streets of attractive architecture and some impressive old churches. Everything is within easy reach and you should be able to sightsee without feeling jaded, despite the steep climb up Costa de Ses Voltes. There are lots of coffee and beer stops, and some smart shops to peer into, and if you choose to walk in the morning, the fish market and the stalls within Claustre del Carme will still be open.

Time: A leisurely 3 hours. Distance: 1.5km (1 mile).

Start your trip from the tourist office on the quayside at the bottom of Costa de Ses Voltes. Cross the road in front of the office and prepare for a climb.

1 Costa de Ses Voltes

This is Costa de Ses Voltes, the grand entrance to the old town of Maó. The winding street is cut through with a broad flight of steps and finished with manicured greenery to replace the cobbled ramp that the British built to move cargo and men up into the town. *Climb the steps and when you reach the top (Plaça d'Espanya, see pp45–6), turn left and cross the street. To your left is the fish market.*

2 Peixeteria (Fish Market)

The market was built in Modernist style (*see pp46–7*) in the 1920s on the remains of a bastion from the Renaissance city walls. This is a great place to take in the atmosphere as locals shop for supper. *From the market doorway turn left and the Església del Carme is directly ahead.*

3 Mercat Claustre del Carme

Built in the 18th-century, Església del Carme is the largest church in the city. The adjoining cloisters house the fruit and vegetable market and a tasteful shopping centre with quality stalls, as well as upstairs exhibitions and the Hernández Mora Museum (*see p39*). *Retrace your path across the square and when you reach the top of the Ses Voltes turn left up the narrow Portal de Mar. At the next intersection turn right into Plaça de la Constitució and the entrance to Església de Santa Maria is on the right.*

4 Església de Santa Maria

The interior of the church has a minimalist nave which contrasts with a Baroque altar and side chapels. There are regular organ recitals in the church daily at 11.30am from April to October (*see p40*). *From the doorway of the church turn right and you will find yourself in the ornate Ajuntament (town hall, north of the square).*

5 Ajuntament

The Ajuntament was built in 1613 (*see p37*) and the original structure was given a Baroque facelift in the following century. The main meeting rooms have colourful period décor.
Turn right out of the town hall and carry on until you hit Carrer d'Isabel II. Go straight on and you will walk past the Gobierno Militar building on the right before the Església de Sant Francesc appears ahead.

6 Església de Sant Francesc

Completed in 1752 (*see p40*), parts of the interior are covered in intricate floral decoration.
Next door is the Museu de Menorca.

7 Museu de Menorca

The island's showcase of archaeological and historical artefacts lies in its Talayotic remains, but there are also fascinating ancient Egyptian, Roman and Punic exhibits on display here (*see pp42–5*). Enjoy the Baroque cloisters that were built as part of the Franciscan monastery complex.
Turn right and take Carrer des Frares to the intersection on Carrer s'Arraval one block ahead. Turn left and you will see the Port de St Roc further down the street.

8 Port de St Roc

This is the last remaining section of the medieval city wall (*see p47*).

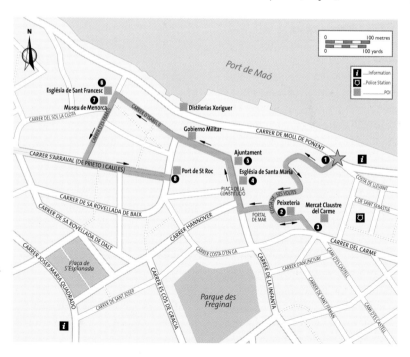

Maó harbour

The magnificent inlet that serves Maó has been a focal point for seafarers over the centuries. Where once fleets of naval military ships plied the waters, today you can see an army of pleasure boats. Five kilometres (3 miles) long and up to one kilometre (²/₃ mile) wide in places, the harbour holds several attractions along its shores, and a number of companies offer boat trips from here. It is also lined with buzzing bars, clubs, cafés and restaurants. See p62 for map of Maó harbour.

This is still a commercial port with a few industrial works, shipyards and the commercial docks situated inland from the city on the south side of the inlet. Day-trippers can take boat cruises from the main dock in the heart of Maó (*see p62*), while the pleasure cruisers and yachts line the quayside to the east of the town along Moll de Llevant.

The entrance to the harbour was first fortified in the mid-16th century when the Ottoman threat from the east was at its height and both Maó and Ciutadella were attacked. Castell de Sant Felip was a 'state-of-the-art' complex for its time but, in many ways, rather than protecting the population, it increased the value of Menorca to the forces who coveted this safe harbour (*see pp54–5*). When the Spanish destroyed the fort in 1782, they did so to render the place less attractive to other power-brokers.

It was the British Royal Navy who made the inner harbour what it is today. They saw the advantage of this deep sheltered inlet even before they took possession of Menorca, and pushed for landing and watering rights from the Spanish Crown in the 1660s.

As rivalries between the European powers continued, helped by dynastic wrangling across the continent, it became imperative for the Royal Navy to secure a safe passage through the Mediterranean. Menorca was one of a series of staging posts from Gibraltar to Malta that gave Britain leverage in many pan-European disputes and power struggles.

While the city of Maó was allowed to develop relatively organically – in response to the administrative duties of the capital bestowed upon it by the British in 1722 (and the resulting economic opportunities) – other areas of the inlet were totally restructured to accommodate warships and the huge garrison needed to cater to this massive fleet.

Supplies were of paramount importance. Fresh food needed to be transported from the island's interior, stored and loaded. The wooden ships needed constant attention and repair, so dry docks were needed. Meanwhile, smiths would be hard at work making horseshoes for the ground transport, nails for the ships and repairing the hoops of barrels.

The final decision that had to be taken was where to keep the supplies of cannon and gunpowder that the naval guns needed in times of war. The British chose a site on the north shore of the island and erected a large and secure arsenal with waterside access in the shape of a polygon, incorporating the small harbour island of de Pinto to complete the structure. Today it is not possible to visit the arsenal but you can get a good view of the buildings and the layout on the Maó harbour boat cruise (*see pp62–3*).

The inlet was a popular subject for Menorcan painters, and the changing landscape along the harbour through the different eras can be viewed in the Museu de Menorca (*see pp42–5*) in Maó.

Cala de Sant Esteve

One of the longest, narrowest and least spoilt coves on the island, Sant Esteve gives a glimpse of what most of Menorca looked like before development. Small houses cling limpet-like to the water line; tiny fishing boats lie moored on the

The harbour plays host to pleasure cruisers and yachts

shoreline or tied in the centre of the watercourse; children play football along the single lane that runs around the brightly coloured houses; and on Sundays families get together for a long barbecue lunch and afternoon siesta.

The entrance to the exhibition at Fort Marlborough (*see pp55–7*) is here, near the far end of the village (although it is not signposted as such on the approach into the cove), while the remains of Fort St Phillip (*see pp54–5*) are set above its north shore.

Sant Esteve was given its name because it is believed that certain relics of St Stephen were landed here; it is said that these relics proved so powerful that their very presence on the island caused a large number of the Jewish population to convert to Catholicism.

Es Castell

Built by the British, Es Castell was a garrison town erected in the mid-18th century when the Royal Navy arrived for the second time. Set on a sheltered harbour on the south shore, the garrison, then called Georgetown after King George III, sat in the protective shadow of Fort St Phillip, a couple of kilometres away to the southeast, which the Royal Navy used to full advantage. Fort Marlborough was erected to counter the changing technology of naval armaments during the mid-18th century. During the first occupation, the British had made do with a smaller garrison, S'Arraval Nova, which had grown around Fort St

Phillip, but this was not large enough. At the height of the British presence, the place would have been bustling with tattooed sailors taking the 'King's shilling', plus an administrative team, station personnel and their families. When the British left, the compound was taken over by the Spanish and life continued pretty much like this for Es Castell until the end of the Franco era in the 1970s.

Today, on the face of it, there are few reminders of the founding of the town. Rows of whitewashed family houses line the streets and there is a relaxed atmosphere to the harbourfront. This could be any Menorcan town until you delve a bit deeper. At the top of the town is a large, open square called Plaça de s'Esplanada. Aside from Plaça d'es Born in Ciutadella (*see pp126–8*), this is the biggest on the island and was once a parade ground for the military; now it is lined with bars and cafés and there is a children's playground in the middle. All the buildings flanking the square were built as part of the original garrison headquarters. Homogeneous in style, they were the heart and soul of British military life on the island, with every decision taken by bewigged officers in these buildings.

One side of the quadrangle houses the Town Hall, with its distinctive red façade, while another has a small military collection. The artefacts, models and paintings in the **Museu Militar** (*Plaça s'Esplanada; tel: 971 36 21 00; www.museomilitarmenorca.com;*

Overlooking the harbour in Es Castell

The Town Hall at Es Castell

open: Mon & Thur 11am–1pm; admission charge) help in the understanding of the island's complex military history.

Head down to the seafront and you can still see the attraction of the location to naval planners. Set around the two broad inlets of Cala Corb and Cales Fonts, the access was redesigned by the British to offer easy docking and maximum protection for the vessels. Today, the harbourside is home to a busy squadron of small fishing boats, and the dockside buildings house cafés and shops. The only obvious reminder of the military is a single tower on the north side of Cales Fonts. Es Castell is known for its seafood restaurants and it is the place where people from Maó come for a relaxed lunch away from the tourist crowds that pack the port's eateries.

Castell de Sant Felip (Fort St Phillip)

It is difficult to fully appreciate the impact that the building of Fort St Phillip had on Menorca's reputation in the eyes of European leaders. Built in the mid-16th century on the orders of Charles V, Holy Roman Emperor and the most powerful man of his era, the fort was meant as a deterrent against the Ottomans – but it added value to Maó's natural harbour and made it more attractive to other European nations because it could now be defended (*see p50*).

Fort St Phillip stood on the south bank of the inlet with flanks out both to the west and east over the sea approaches. There is little left of the original structure as it was destroyed by the Spanish when they retook the island in the late 18th century. However, the site remained strategically important and it is still a military area today. On the ground it is possible to make out scant sections of what would have been massive curtain walls and arrow-shaped rivets. Go to the Museu Militar in

Es Castell (*see pp52–4*) for models and paintings of the fort.

Beneath the ground there are artillery placements in corridors and galleries where the garrison was housed. The labyrinth was extended over the decades with each new colonial overlord, and it is much larger than its cousin, Fort Marlborough (*see below*). During the siege of 1782, it is said that over 3,500 English personnel and their families were holed up here for six months. *www.museomilitarmenorca.com. Guided visits are available but times vary throughout the year; check the website for details. Night-time torch-lit tours also take place from June to September. Admission charge.*

Fuerte de Marlborough (Fort Marlborough)

When the British took control of Menorca in the early years of the 18th

The impregnable Fort Marlborough

The reconstructed Martello tower at Fort Marlborough

century, they realised that the southeastern flank of Fort St Phillip was vulnerable, and that changes to the structure itself would not be adequate. Instead, they decided to build a totally independent fortification incorporating the latest advances in military design. It was named Fort Marlborough after Sir John Churchill, Duke of Marlborough, who was the most noted military man of the era.

The basis for the impregnability of the fort was that it was built underground, cut out of rock, with access from Cala de Sant Esteve (*see pp51–2*). Work started in 1710 and was completed in the mid-1720s. The fort suffered two attacks: from the French in 1756 and the Spanish in 1781. On both occasions the garrison eventually capitulated but only after prolonged sieges that diverted the attackers'

attention from other targets. The small garrison of 65 men and a commander cost the enemy a lot more men, time and valuable resources.

From the outside, the structure seems simple, with a featureless mound (once the site of gunnery placements) surrounded by a moat that held water. Towards the end of the 18th century, during the final British occupation, a Martello tower – the Stuart or Penjat Tower – was added atop a nearby bluff. The interior, however, is a maze of seemingly endless tunnels leading off a main bore. The fort museum, set in the underground chambers, has some good high-tech displays (not forgetting rowdy explosions) and audiovisual exhibits to explain the history of the building. History buffs will enjoy learning about the sieges and military action that took place here as part of a pan-European power game in the late 18th and early 19th centuries.

Head out on the point above the fort to the Martello tower for views across the mouth of Maó inlet and the remains of Fort St Phillip and Fortalesa Isabel II (*see pp58–9*).
Fort Marlborough. Cala de Sant Esteve. Tel: 971 36 04 62. Open: Tue–Sat 9am–1pm & 3–7pm, Sun 9.30am–1pm. Admission charge.

Golden Farm

This handsome colonial mansion, officially known as Sant Antoni, sits high on the north bank of the inlet. It is thought that the house was Lord Nelson's billet when he was in charge of the naval company here for a short time during the 1798–1802 British occupation of the island. At the time, rumours of his affair with Lady Hamilton were rife and locals were sure that she joined him here to carry on their illicit relationship. However, it is highly unlikely that she travelled to Menorca, let alone stayed with Nelson at the mansion. Nelson himself was rarely here, being much more concerned about the fate of the Hamilton family in Naples on the Italian west coast. He even refused to return to the island when it was under threat from French naval forces in 1799. The house is not open to the public. The best views of it are from a harbour cruise (*see pp62–3*).

A mobile artillery piece at Fortalesa Isabel II

A view over Fortalesa Isabel II at La Mola

La Mola

La Mola is the general term for the nub of land that occupies the far northeastern corner of the inlet at the mouth of the harbour. Just as on the south shore, this area was important strategic military land, and it is covered with fortifications. **Fortalesa Isabel II**, built here by the Spanish in the 18th century, had little military value but added to national confidence. It was a feared political prison throughout Franco's regime and for decades was off-limits to the public, before being reopened to great aplomb in the early 2000s.

The fort was built to counter a specific threat in the 1840s. The British had a strong presence in the Mediterranean and the French were expanding into North Africa. Between these two powers lay the Balearics, and the Spanish felt that either might take the islands.

Military planners did not account for the advancements in artillery, and as the castle took 25 years to build it was outdated before it was finished.

The fort was named after Queen Isabel II in honour of her visit to the garrison soon after it was completed. Once through the impressive entrance, a series of numbered panels offers information about the fortifications, the bulk of which face southwest overlooking the approaches from the Maó inlet. The hornwork and redoubt at the southwest corner are the most impressive features, with strong sturdy walls and small holes at every gunning placement. There are views across the inlet to the capital from here.

Fortalesa Isabel II has impressive underground galleries leading to gunning placements in the curtain walls. The **Loop-holed Gallery** is a long row of interconnected gunning rooms that must have been extremely claustrophobic and hot for the soldiers on duty. The walking tour leads you directly through the structure.

Out to the eastern section of the fort, emerge into open air and stroll past several modern barracks used in the late 20th century, to reach the Isabel II's tour de force, a 15in Vickers battery gun still embedded in its position. For more details of the fort, see the Fortalesa Isabel II walk (*see pp64–5*). The tour takes about two and a half hours with a lot of walking, but the fort offers a minibus service between the Loop-holed Gallery, the Vickers gun and the ticket office in the afternoons, between 1pm and 3pm.

Much of the rest of La Mola is open ground, and it is a favourite place for locals to come for a spot of fishing. Bring a picnic and find a quiet spot for lunch.

Fishing boat in Maó harbour

The Loop-holed Gallery at Fortalesa Isabel II

*Fortalesa Isabel II. Tel: 971 36 40 40.
www.fortalesamola.com. Open: Jun–Sept
10am–8pm; May & Oct 10am–6pm;
Nov–Apr Tue–Sun 10am–2pm.
Admission charge.
Daily trips from the port at Maó with
Yellow Catamarans (tel: 971 35 23 07;
www.yellowcatamarans.com).*

Llatzeret and the islands

Several islands dot the Maó inlet. The
largest of these is **Illa del Llatzeret**, or
Lazaretto, just inland from La Mola. In
fact the island was attached to the spit
of La Mola until the early 20th century,
when a channel was cut to separate the
two, with the purpose of providing a

safe approach for ships arriving at Fortalesa Isabel II. Llatzeret was the site of a hospital for infectious diseases that looks every bit as imposing as the fortress nearby. The hospital closed in 1917, after which it became a holiday complex for public health workers. Newly refurbished, today it is also a conference centre.

The smallest of the islands, **Illa Quarentena** sits just beside Llatzeret. Officially named Illa Plana, the unofficial name arises because for many years it was a quarantine station where people had to wait a certain length of time (traditionally 40 days,

hence the word quarantine after *quaranta*, the Italian word for forty) to ascertain that they had no communicable diseases. This was a common practice among the island's communities in the wake of the devastating Black Death outbreaks. Later it became the first American base in the Mediterranean.

Finally, there is the **Illa del Rei** or King's Island, so called because Alfonso III landed here in 1287 after he had taken Menorca from the Moors. Illa del Rei is also called 'Bloody Island' because this is the location where the British built their military hospital.

The small island of Illa Quarentena, also known as Illa Plana

Boat tour: Maó harbour

Boats depart daily from the embarkation point opposite the base of the Costa de Ses Voltes for a tour of one of the world's most famous natural harbours. Some companies, such as the Yellow Catamarans (tel: 971 35 23 07; www.yellowcatamarans.com), offer glass-bottom boats so that you can watch the sea life as well as what's happening along the shoreline.

Time: 1¼ hours.
Distance: 10km (6 miles).

1 Moll de Ponent

As your boat begins to move away from the embarkation point at Moll de Ponent, you should be able to see the pleasure yachts lining the quayside to the east, and the landmark that is the Xoriguer Distillery (*see pp38–9*) housed in old portside warehouse buildings to the west.

At the start the boat will first cross to the north bank of the inlet at one of its narrowest points.

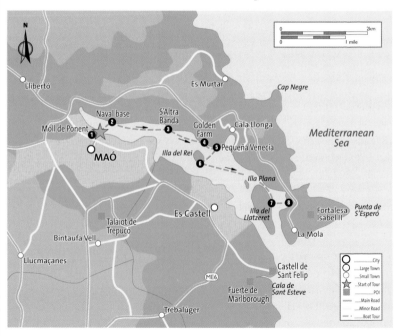

2 The naval base

From here you will get your best view of the old British arsenal and naval base (*see pp50–51*), where all the cannon, gunpowder and other armaments were stored. The compound still maintains its 18th-century layout and the neo-classical buildings still look shipshape.
The boat moves slowly east along the north shore out towards the sea. Just a little way along you will see a point of land jutting out into the inlet.

3 S'Altra Banda

S'Altra Banda was a popular place for the people of Maó to relax. Eventually a number of villas were built here by wealthy families. The most famous buildings are the *banyars de pedra* (bathing houses), built in the 19th century with the lower storeys in the water so that ladies could swim without being seen.
A few minutes further east Golden Farm comes into view.

4 Golden Farm

This fine 18th-century mansion still has an imposing presence today. It is said that Lord Nelson stayed here when he was in charge of the garrison in the 1790s (*see p57*).
Nearby you will notice an unusual whitewashed building.

5 Pequeña Venecia

Pequeña Venecia (Little Venice) is a single whitewashed house sitting on rocks in the shallows along the harbourside. It was so named because,

with its feet in the water, it reminded local people of homes in Venice.
Look away from the coast from here and you will see the port's smallest island to the southeast, Illa del Rei.

6 Illa del Rei

In 1287, Illa del Rei (*see p61*) was pushed centre-stage when Alfonso III landed to proclaim the end of the Islamic era on the island. The British later used it as the site for their military hospital; the Americans arrived in the 1820s.
Move on to the larger island beyond Illa del Rei, Llatzeret.

7 Illa del Llatzeret (Lazaretto)

The buildings here look like fortifications (*see pp60–61*) but they actually housed a hospital for contagious diseases. The walls were built high because it was thought that diseases were carried in the air, and that the walls would contain them inside.
The boat travels on through the narrow artificial channel cut to separate Llatzeret from La Mola in the early 20th century, and you get your first view of Fortalesa Isabel II.

8 La Mola

The fort at La Mola, Fortalesa Isabel II, (*see pp58–61*) on the northern mouth of the Maó inlet looks impressive, but it was built using outdated design and was vulnerable as soon as it was inaugurated in 1852. During Franco's era, it was used as a prison housing the dictator's political enemies.

Walk: Fortalesa Isabel II

Fortalesa Isabel II at La Mola is one of Menorca's major historical attractions. Sections of the huge castle have been spruced up and an excellent multilingual audio accompaniment has been added, offering a historical and architectural background to each of the numbered areas. If you have an interest in castles or forts, you will really enjoy this itinerary.

Time: 2½ hours.
Distance: 3km (2 miles).

1 Queen's Gate

The fort was inaugurated in 1852 and the magnificent entry point at Queen's Gate is one of its finest and most impressive features. Queen Isabel – so far the only female monarch of Spain as it is now understood – visited in 1860 and the castle, originally Fortalesa La Mola, was renamed Fortalesa Isabel II in her honour.

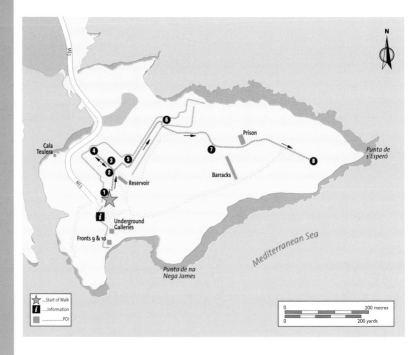

*Once through the gate, the ticket office is
on the left. You can get full details of the
tour here. From the ticket office, the route
leads right down to the southern curtain
walls and subterranean galleries used for
storing gunpowder before heading north
to the hornworks.*

2 Hornworks

The hornworks, with 54 cannon
emplacements, were the fort's last line
of defence.
*Surrounding the hornworks is the
Redoubt.*

3 The Redoubt

The Redoubt – from the Medieval
Latin *reductus* or 'refuge' – is a tiny
'fort within a fort'. The role of this
circular building was to allow the
company somewhere defendable
to retreat to, should the main walls
be breached.
*Walk through the Redoubt and into a
small square. Across the square and up
the ramp is the Coop.*

4 The Coop

The Coop (or *caponera*) was a forward
position facing inland towards Maó
rather than out to sea, as this was
considered the vulnerable flank of the
fort: the seaward side was too rocky to
attack from.
*Retrace your steps past the Redoubt
towards the reservoir. Proceed down the
ramp into the moat of the pincer, a part
of the castle designed to trap attackers
in crossfire.*

5 The moat

The moat is now empty but was once
an integral part of the defences.
*From the base of the moat, follow the
bronze arrows to the Loop-holed or
Artillery Gallery, reached through a
circular tower.*

6 The Loop-holed Gallery

The Loop-holed Gallery is a long line of
gun emplacements linked by a narrow
tunnel. This was the integral defence of
the curtain wall facing Maó, but there is
no view to the outside except through
the gunnery slits in the walls.
*The gallery is several hundred metres
long, after which you emerge into the
open air at the Princess Tower. The route
then heads east across the open land of
La Mola peninsula. After a couple of
minutes you will find the water cistern
on the right.*

7 The Queen's Water Cistern

This huge structure stored water and
could keep the fort self-sufficient for
many weeks in times of siege.
*Continue to walk seaward and you will
reach the final defences.*

8 The Vickers gun

The 15in Vickers gun was added to the
defences during the 20th century. It
represents the development in military
systems and tactics after the 1850s,
when the fort was built.
*Take the path across the headland back to
the ticket office, or wait for the minibus
(1–3pm) to take you back to the start.*

The British in Menorca

When the British gained control of Menorca in 1708, they found an impoverished island struggling to feed itself.

Power was in the hands of a small number of patrician families who cared little for the working population and simply wanted to extract taxes from them.

The plight of the local people was not normally high on the list of priorities of the colonial authorities, but one exceptional individual, Richard Kane, Deputy Governor and then Governor during the first occupation, happened to be the right man in the right place. He saw that there were easy solutions to many of the problems and set about introducing a sea of changes that would have an immense effect on the lives of the ordinary people. Kane's actions were not always altruistic because he had a British garrison to manage and feed. However, he left behind 'a legacy of justice and honour' where there had been none, according to his biographer Janet Sloss, and he is still remembered with fondness by Menorcans.

Firstly, Kane assessed Menorca's poor-quality animal stock and had healthy Friesian cattle shipped out from the UK; without these, it is debatable whether Menorcan cheese (*see pp116–17*) would ever have achieved the quality it has today. He also ordered new seed stock to replenish the poor crops for both fodder and human food, and drained the marshes in the river basin close to Maó to increase the acreage of good-quality soil close to his garrison headquarters.

Another area he tackled was the poor transport infrastructure on the island. There was no main route linking the major towns and it was impossible to transport goods, even fresh crops, from the hinterland. Kane commissioned a road – known as Camí d'en Kane – to link Maó with Ciutadella on the west coast for the first time.

Fresh water was also an issue. Although many of the buildings were designed to capture rainwater, there was no communal facility and there were frequent outbreaks of disease due to the lack of fresh water for drinking and washing. Kane approved the building of a huge cistern close to the town of Es Mercadal in the centre of the island, and paid for it himself.

The British barracks in Es Castell

The second and third periods of British occupation, however, were far less constructive. General Johnston, who was Governor between 1763 and 1782, was a strident authoritarian, and his hard-handedness soured what had in the earlier years been a mutually beneficial relationship.

Richard Kane

Richard Kane was born in Ireland in about 1662 and made military service his life, reaching the rank of Brigadier General. He was singularly successful as a commander under the Duke of Marlborough, and wrote a training and tactics manual that was highly influential for decades.

The prestigious job in Menorca was a just reward for his loyalty and organisational skill. Though he was temporarily transferred to manage the defence of Gibraltar against a Spanish force in the 1720s, he returned to Menorca and was still in office on the island when he died in 1736.

For more details on the life of Kane, get hold of a copy of *Richard Kane: First Governor of Menorca* by Janet Sloss, available from The Bonaventura Press: *www.bonaventura.co.uk*

Southeastern Menorca

The compact region to the south of the capital has some of the prettiest landscapes on the island. Neat whitewashed traditional llocs *(farms) sit among rolling land surrounded by vines and carpeted with vibrant bougainvillea. The ancient Menorcans loved it here too, and some of their most dramatic legacies are to be found hidden behind high stone walls or standing sentinel in fields at the roadside.*

This is a prosperous agricultural area of the Balearics, but also provides some of the most upmarket tourist development in small *calas* around the mostly rocky coast. Resorts like Punta Prima and S'Algar on the east coast provide the focus for boat trips and diving schools, and offer a choice of restaurants and bars. On the south coast a string of small and low-key resorts lines the bays. The rocky coastline backed by mature pines and dotted with villas is exceptionally alluring.

A string of small hamlets – the 'Binis' – sits just inland from the coast. You will pass from one to the other without really noticing the boundaries, and each has a route leading down to the southeastern coast.

This small region is easy to explore by car, but the gentle undulations also offer excellent cycling along roads of a good standard. Everything is easy to find and within close proximity, and it is only around 20 minutes from Maó.

Basílica des Fornàs de Torelló

This rather underwhelming ruin is one of very few early Christian sites left in Menorca and, as such, forms an important architectural site. Most of the others were destroyed by the Vandals who, although also Christians, were an Arian sect who had different beliefs from the mainstream Christian tenets of worship. Built in the 5th or early 6th century, the basilica stands on the site of an impressive late Roman villa. The original Roman mosaic floors

Talaiot de Torellónet Vell

were incorporated into the church and make a tremendous impact. The overall quality of the work is high and includes scenes featuring influences from Roman Africa, plus verdant foliage and peacocks. Close to the nave there is a scene depicting two lions facing the tree of life. Of the church, only the base plan of the three original aisles and the apse are in situ but this allows you to envisage the overall floor plan. It is amazing to think that the whole building remained undiscovered until 1956.

Close by is the **Talaiot de Torellónet Vell**, the highest ancient structure on the island with walls of finely chiselled stone. The tower is the only one to sport a window, but archaeologists have a theory that this was a later addition. It has now been usurped by the airport authorities and is equipped with high-tech equipment to facilitate landings and takeoffs. The surrounding land was

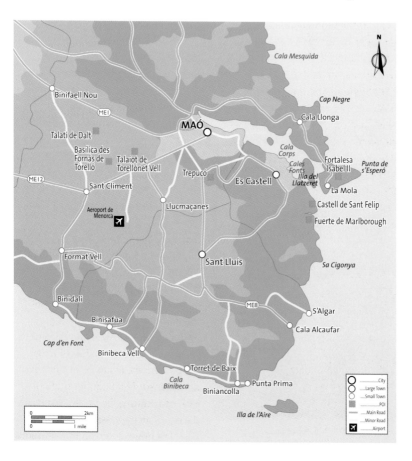

◯	City
◯	Large Town
○	Small Town
◼	POI
—	Main Road
	Minor Road
✈	Airport

the site of a Bronze Age smelting plant. Archaeologists have discovered remains of the equipment and shards of molten metal plus a small statue that may have been a ritual object.

Basílica des Fornás de Torelló. Off the link road between the ME1 and the Maó/Sant Climent Road, close to the airport. www.menorcatour.com. Open: 24 hours. Free admission.

Binibeca Vell

This award-winning development on the south coast is one of the turning points in the tourist market on Menorca. A whitewashed Mediterranean 'fishing village' of low-rise hotels and apartment complexes designed by Spanish architect Antonio Sintes, the concept was to re-create the lines and features of a traditional

The whitewashed 'village' of Binibeca Vell

village while incorporating 21st-century holiday accommodation. The design plan, with its soft lime-washed walls, stone steps, archways, wooden balconies and a mass of verdant landscaping, enhances the landscape rather than detracting from it, and the complex seems to tumble down the hillside into the azure water of Caló d'es Fust with its rocky outcrops.

When it was conceived and built, Binibeca Vell was a major departure from the high-rise accommodation that predominated in Spain in the 1970s. The success of the concept helped Menorca shift emphasis to the high-quality, low-rise accommodation that has sprung up around the coast.

The tiny village is a pleasure to explore. The narrow alleyways lead to small cottages, each with a colourful door or terrace replete with local ceramics or a sleepy cat; there is a wealth of detail to discover around every whitewashed corner, including traditional chimneys. Every building has something a little different.

Perhaps the only downside here is the lack of a decent stretch of sand to lay out your towel. Much of the sunning and bathing is done on rocks or concrete lidos, although there is a great sandy beach with lots of room for everyone at Binibeca Nou just to the east.

Binisafua

The *taula* (T-shaped stone monument) on the road into Binisafua from Maó is a single-feature site but it sits in one of the

A quiet corner in the tiny cove at Binisafua

prettiest parts of the island and doesn't require any walking from the car park. Enjoy the cluster of renovated whitewashed traditional *llocs* (farms); some are holiday homes for British and German expats; others are excellent agrotourism complexes; and the rest remain a vibrant working part of the rural lifestyle. Make your way to the minute beach here for a quiet afternoon of catching the sun.
At the southern junction of the Llucmaçanes road and the road north from Binibeca Vell.

Punta Prima

One of the two main tourist developments in the southeast, Punta Prima is set in the very southeastern corner of Menorca. The resort has a range of holiday hotels, bars and some long stretches of sandy beach, and is popular with those who want the action of Maó close at hand. The choppy seas on this part of the island attract Menorca's windsurfers, but swimming can be dangerous if you venture too far from the shore because of the deep currents between the land and the barren Illa de l'Aire offshore.

There is a flag system in operation; red means don't swim! Over the centuries, the dangerous waters have resulted in numerous shipwrecks that now make excellent diving sites.

Fishing boats in Binisafua

S'Algar

Along with Punta Prima, S'Algar provides much of the holiday accommodation in the region and has been established since the earliest days of tourism on the island. Here this tends to be family villas set in cottage gardens, predictable but better than faceless high-rise towers. The resort faces south on a sheltered bay and has a reasonable swimming beach. The prettier resort of Cala Alcaufar lies less than a kilometre (½ mile) south around the coast. It is set around a narrow curved inlet protected by the remains of a stone tower, and has less development and more character.

From S'Algar, take an easy walk (around 1½ hrs) to Barranco de Rafalet, where the rocky outcrops offer some fine views.

Sant Climent

This tiny town was founded in 1817 on the site of a 13th-century chapel commissioned by Jaume II, and it is now unfortunately in the final approach path of the airport. Not a place to spend your whole holiday, and of the original chapel there is no sign, but stop for a while to admire the neo-Gothic replacement erected in 1889. It's also well worth visiting for a great restaurant (*see p171*) and an island-famous jazz venue (*see p153*).

The village also has one of the last remaining *el cos* roads – an extra-wide section of town road used for horse and donkey races. At various points along the track you will see narrow steps up the sides of the stone walls, which allowed the spectators to climb to the top for a better view. A plaque in Spanish marks the site.

El cos, at the start of the route to Binidalí. Open access. Free admission.

Sant Lluís

Built by the French when they took the island in 1756, Sant Lluís was a military town and erected according to the new principles of town planning on a grid of straight streets and 90° intersections, totally different from the organic expansion of the older settlements on the island with their narrow curved alleyways. The original town consisted of 18 blocks but the modern town has expanded well beyond this. The predominantly Breton sailors of the French fleet were garrisoned here under the Count of Lannion. Today, although many of the buildings have been replaced, some of the original buildings line the routes that lead to Carrer de Sant Lluís, the main thoroughfare. The town's neoclassical parish church was consecrated to the canonised Louis IX, after whom the town is also named. He played a pre-eminent role in the Crusades during the 13th century.

However, there are few other reminders of the French presence here. The town's **Museu Etnológic** (Ethnology Museum) is housed in the Molí de Dalt, a renovated 18th-century windmill, and it concentrates on local lifestyle and traditional practices. You will find a range of interesting old farm implements and other tools plus some pretty traditional costumes in the ethnological section. The mill was restored in 1987 and the machinery is still in working order.

The parish church with a neoclassical façade in Sant Lluís

The windmill (Molí de Dalt) in Sant Lluís now houses the Ethnology Museum

Museu Etnológic. Carrer de Sant Lluís.
Tel: 971 15 10 84. Open: Mon–Fri
10am–2pm & 6–8pm, Sat–Sun
10am–1pm. Admission charge.

Talatí de Dalt

One of Menorca's major Talayotic remains, Talatí de Dalt is the best preserved of its ancient sites. It has been thoroughly excavated since 1997 and has yielded a vast amount of information for archaeologists.

The settlement is now thought to have had a population of around 100 people in its heyday, around the 3rd century BC, when it was an important trading town with links to Carthage. It was well populated until the Romans took the island in the 2nd century BC and continued to offer shelter throughout the first millennium until the Moorish rout in the 13th century, but by that time it had been in decline for a few centuries and constituted little more than meagre accommodation for humans or animals.

The structures here form a loose semicircle surrounded by the remains of an original megalithic curtain wall. The site includes natural and artificial caves used, it is thought, as burial chambers or reliquaries, and a number of Talayotic houses of varying sizes, some with sophisticated hypostyle

The ancient site of Talatí de Dalt

chambers and flagstone roofs. One house was found to have domestic artefacts dating from the middle of the Talayotic period through the Phoenician and Roman influences with a layer of shards of Arabic pottery at the top – taking us through the whole gamut of civilisation at the site.

The whole complex is fascinating to anyone with an interest in ancient history. The two main attractions for the lay person are the huge main *talaiot* or stone tower (made of finely worked trapezoid stones) and the impressive *taula*, surrounded by a wall of standing stones. This was used for rituals that have yet to be fully explained.

4km (2½ miles) west of Maó just south of the ME1. No telephone. Open: daily 9am–sunset. Admission charge.

Torret de Baix

A small tourist resort, part of the Binibeca Vell line of small resorts, is

The *taula* at Talatí de Dalt

based around the remains of an old stone tower. The small inlet in the resort still has a handful of traditional waterside Menorcan fishermen's houses with rooms above for the family and a basement for the two- or three-man boat with a concrete or stone ramp leading into the water. This inlet, with its pine trees and lido bathing, is one of the most photographed on the island.

Trepucó

It is known that Trepucó was a large Talayotic settlement and an important trading centre close to the inlet at Maó. Today, however, the excavated site is a smaller site than the one at Talatí de Dalt (*see pp75–6*). The quality of the buildings here makes up for the lack of quantity, and the site is well worth visiting. The dramatic *taula* is probably the finest on the island with a single supporting stone of 4.2m (14ft), and it is surrounded, in close proximity, by a circle of other buildings whose walls rise to at least waist level. There are two

Talayotic remains at Trepucó

talaiots on the site but the larger one suffered at the hands of the French who put a gun emplacement on top of it. The French also built characteristic arrowhead curtain walls around the tower – state-of-the-art fortifications at that time.

Archaeologists believe that there were four towers in ancient times. However, the other two are probably field walls or farm buildings today.

1.5km (1 mile) south of Maó. No telephone. Open: Apr & Oct Tue–Sun 9am–3pm; May–Sept Tue–Sat 9am–8pm, Sun–Mon 9am–3pm. Closed Nov–Mar. Admission charge.

HAPPY LANDINGS

When extensions were made to Menorca airport in the wake of the development of mass tourism, some ancient remains had to be moved or destroyed in the process. Just beside the airport terminal is Biniparratxet Petit, excavated and moved to its present site in 1995. The reconstruction is of a complete Talayotic house with a hypostyle chamber. The numerous finds excavated at the time are now housed in the Museum of Menorca (*see pp42–5*).

Southeastern Menorca

Drive: Southeastern Menorca

This quiet corner of the island, a combination of the ancient and the modern, has some excellent coastal scenery and lots of places to stop and admire the view, have a drink or enjoy a leisurely lunch.

Time: 4 hours.
Distance: 36km (22 miles).

Start from the centre of Maó following signs for Es Castell. This is signposted directly from the centre of town; find the outer ring road and travel east.

1 Es Castell

Take in the little town's historic significance at the military museum (*see pp52–4*) and wander along the seafront at Cales Fonts (*see p54*). You'll find plenty of cafés to stop for coffee.
Return to the outer ring road at Maó. Turn left and then left again at the next roundabout. You are now on the ME8 to Sant Lluís, 5km (3 miles) ahead.

2 Sant Lluís

Sant Lluís is a military town founded by the French. Enjoy the parish church and the Ethnology Museum housed in the town's old windmill (*see pp73–5*).
Leave Sant Lluís travelling south out of town on the ME8 in the direction of Cala Alcaufar and Punta Prima. After 2km (1¼ miles) the road splits; take the right fork to Punta Prima.

3 Punta Prima

Punta Prima is a well-established resort with a vast stretch of sandy beach (*see p71*). Just offshore is the Illa de l'Aire, now a protected nature reserve. You can take a short boat trip here or walk along the coast. There are also bars and restaurants if it is hitting lunchtime.
Leave Punta Prima travelling west following signs for Biniancolla and Binibeca Vell along the main coast road. Travel on with the sea on your left. The route runs past some pretty tiny inlets with concrete bathing lidos and the occasional traditional fisherman's cottage set against the water's edge. After 4km (2½ miles) you'll reach Binibeca Vell.

4 Binibeca Vell

This award-winning mock-Mediterranean fishing village was a benchmark in Menorca's approach to tourist development. Enjoy exploring its architecture and narrow alleyways and while away an hour in Los Bucaneros beach bar.

Leave the resort by continuing west along the coast road through Binisafua and Cap d'en Font. At around 6km (4 miles) from Binibeca Vell, the road turns inland and it is then 4.5km (2¾ miles) to Sant Climent.

5 Sant Climent

The neo-Gothic church erected in 1889 dominates this little town, which has one of the last remaining *el cos* roads in Menorca – a section of town road used

for horse and donkey races (*see pp72–3*). *Leave Sant Climent travelling north. Hit the main road ME1 and turn left, then right at the signpost to Rafal Rubi.*

6 Rafal Rubi

The Rafal Rubi site has twin *navetas* (*see p83 & p111*) in a farmer's field just off the main road. *From here return to the main ME1 road and turn left back to Maó.*

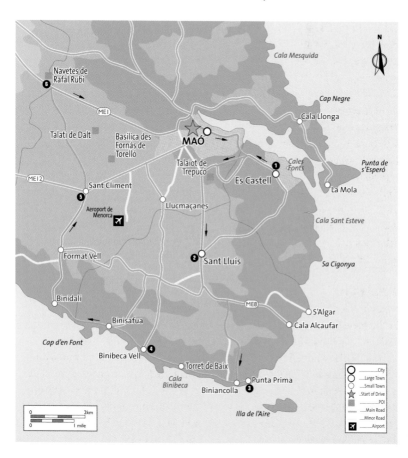

Drive: Discovering Menorca's ancient past

Wandering from one ancient site to another makes for a great day of exploration. You will find yourself in a whole range of locations and environments, and you will be able to take in the full gamut of Menorca's differing landscapes before ending up in Ciutadella in time for supper.

Time: 7 hours.
Distance: 110km (68 miles).

Leave Maó heading south following signs for Talaiot de Trepucó. This is not signposted directly from the centre of town, but find the outer ring road and if travelling east towards Es Castell turn right at the next roundabout after the Sant Lluís roundabout. The site is 1.5km (1 mile) down this narrow lane.

1 Talaiot de Trepucó

This dramatic *taula* is probably the finest on the island (*see p77*), with a single supporting stone of 4.2m (14ft).

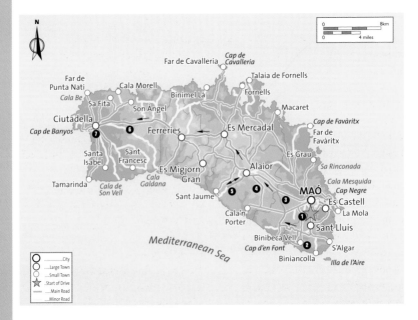

Leave the site and retrace your drive to the ring road at Maó. Turn left and then left again at the next roundabout. You are now on the ME8 to Sant Lluís, 5km (3 miles) ahead. Once there, follow signs for Binibeca Vell out to the southwest, but instead of taking the coast road, drive 150m (165yds) further on, where you will find the site of Binisafua on the right.

2 Binisafua

Binisafua offers a single *taula* (*see* pp70–71) and typical Menorcan countryside.

Leave Binisafua by the narrow cross-country lane running to the east of the site directly north to Llucmaçanes. In the village, take the left fork, signposted Sant Climent. When you reach the Maó/Sant Climent road after 1.5km (1 mile), turn left, then right at the next large roundabout. After 1.5km (1 mile) you will reach the ME1. Take the Ciutadella direction. After 2.5km (1¹/₂ miles) you will see a sign left to Talatí de Dalt.

3 Talatí de Dalt

This Neolithic settlement had a population of around 100 people in its heyday. The *taula* is the only one on the island to be supported by a second stone T, and one house was found to have domestic artefacts from the middle of the Talayotic period (*see* pp75–6).

Return to the ME1 and continue in the direction of Ciutadella. After 6.5km (4 miles) take the first Alaior exit off the bypass and turn south on to a country lane with signposts to Cala'n Porter. After

4km (2¹/₂ miles) the signs for Torralba d'en Salort will come into view.

4 Torralba d'en Salort

Torralba d'en Salort was a village with the biggest *taula* in Menorca (*see* p115), plus caves excavated to house bodies, houses and a quarry.

Retrace your route to the Alaior bypass and continue on towards Ciutadella for 1km (²/₃ mile). Take the first turning on the left and carry on for 3km (2 miles) to Torre d'en Galmés, on the left.

5 Torre d'en Galmés

It's a ten-minute walk along a dusty track to this massive but broken *taula*, three well-preserved *talaiots* (circular watchtowers) and an ingenious water collection system. At one time, this 'village' was home to 1,000 people (*see* pp114–15).

Return to the ME1 to continue towards Ciutadella. You are almost on the outskirts when the car park for Naveta des Tudons appears on the left.

6 Naveta des Tudons

Naveta des Tudons is a spectacular single *naveta* (*see* p83) some 200m (220yds) off the main road (*see* pp128–9).

Return to the ME1 by turning right out of the site and then right again at the next crossroads.

7 Ciutadella

After a hard day's ancient-sightseeing, head 6km (4 miles) into Ciutadella and relax with a drink at the harbour.

Ancient Menorca

Menorca was densely populated during ancient times and these people have left a vast legacy, principally in the form of stone structures that are now yielding their secrets to archaeologists. Some of the sites were used long after the ancient civilisations had disappeared, and show traces through the first millennium into medieval times. Many others were used as animal shelters until the advent of the science of archaeology.

Naveta des Tudons near Ciutadella

THE CLASSIFICATION

The scientific community has now separated the development of early Menorcan society into separate eras. Before 1300 BC the population is known as pre-Talayotic I and pre-Talayotic II, and after that date as Talayotic. The Talayotic era lasted until the arrival of the Romans in 123 BC.

The pre-Talayotic people

The earliest remains so far studied have been dated 2500 BC, and until 1800 BC these have been grouped as pre-Talayotic I, relating to the Chalcolithic geological era. These people lived in stone huts, and adapted caves for use as settlements and hypogea (burial chambers). The caves at Cales Coves (*see p104*) and Cala Morell (*see pp120–21*) show the level of skill achieved by the 'cave dwellers'.

From 1800 BC to 1300 BC, the Early Bronze Age, the people are known as pre-Talayotic II and the main difference was development of the burial chambers from the pre-Talayotic I time.

The Talayotic people

From 1500 BC, the Middle and Late Bronze Age, the people are known as Talayotic. This era witnessed the development of the stone mega-structures and village communities we can visit today, and were typified by elongated stone burial chambers.

TALAYOTIC STRUCTURES
Talaiot

The *talaiot*, which is omnipresent on the island (and on neighbouring Mallorca), has given its name to this race of people. These high (up to 10m/33ft) conical towers were built with large, rough stones that stood at

The *taula* at Torre d'en Galmés

the highest point of the village. The exact purpose of the towers has yet to be ascertained, but they could have offered protection to the village in times of danger, or acted as a meeting house for community elders. There are over 200 *talaiots* in Menorca and many more may have existed but the stones were recycled in later eras, including three at Torre d'en Galmés (*see pp114–15*).

Taula

The word *taula* means 'table' in Catalan. Standing at least shoulder height, with some up to 4m (13ft) high, these huge flat stones supported by one or more stone uprights were certainly not used as tables. Researchers believe that they were ritual areas, each surrounded by a horseshoe-shaped stone wall. The latest theory is that these were a representation of a bull's head – the bull being a revered animal all across the Mediterranean basin in ancient times. The archaeological find of the bronze statue at Torralba d'en Salort (*see p81 and p115*), home of Menorca's biggest *taula*, would support this.

Naveta

Single constructions with no surrounding buildings, these huge rough-hewn stone mounds had interior chambers that acted as collective ossuaries. The bones of generations of Talayotic people were laid to rest in these with their precious objects. The artefacts found in *navetas* across the island have added a great deal to our knowledge and respect for these people. The finest example is the Naveta des Tudons (*see p81 and pp128–9*) just east of Ciutadella.

Northern Menorca

Menorca's northern region, the Tramuntana, is its wild land, swept by old northern winds from central Spain. It is slightly cooler than the south in summer and battered by storms in winter. Its vegetation is always low-growing and sometimes non-existent, with several lunar-type landscapes adding drama to the island's diverse geographical palette.

The north has all of Menorca's 'high' ground with three peaks reaching heights of 250m (820ft), although it is generally characterised by rolling hills and a serrated coastline of inlets and rocky peninsulas thrusting out into the Mediterranean.

It is the feeling of a wild and windswept region that is the major draw here. Much of the land is covered by the protective covenants of the Parc Naturel de S'Albufera des Grau (now the subject of massive conservation efforts, *see pp92–5*) so that development will be kept to a minimum. Nestled between the headlands are majestic untamed beaches and marshlands that welcome regular spring and autumn visitors in the form of migrating birds.

The north sees fewer visitors than the verdant migjorn with its picturesque *barrancas* (small valleys) or the west

A marina full of yachts at Addaia

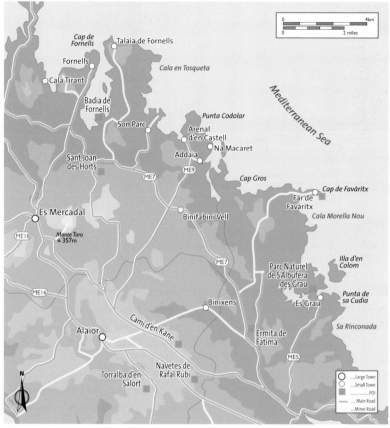

with its family resorts, though Son Parc attracts its share of golfers, and Arenal d'en Castell can match any resort for holiday fun. Windsurfers and kite-surfers flock to the bay at upmarket Fornells for the excellent wind conditions, alongside gourmands who sate their appetites on the best cuisine in Menorca, particularly *caldereta de llagosta* (lobster stew), the local speciality. The walking and hiking trails of the natural park are a perfect way for working off a heavy lunch. Head out from any of the coastal towns or villages and before long you will reach your own private sheltered cove for a spot of swimming or sunbathing.

Addaia

Once the island's most picturesque pleasure port, the cala at Addaia has developed into a fully formed but low-key resort sprawling uphill with rows of holiday villas that are busy in season but a bit of a ghost town in winter. Just north of the bay is Na Macaret, a

Speedboats for hire from the marina at Fornells Bay

favoured inlet for Menorcan town-dwellers who head out here in the summer from Maó and Ciutadella. There are few trappings of mass tourism but there is a popular marina full of yachts from all over southern Spain.

Arenal d'en Castell

The north coast's largest resort, Arenal d'en Castell is set around a wonderful horseshoe-shaped bay protected by two rocky spits that come together like crab claws just offshore. The beach has fine sand and calm waters that are great for kids but the land behind climbs steeply, which means lots of steps up and down to the beach.

There is a low-rise holiday complex reminiscent of Binibeca Vell (*see p70*) rising from the beach in the centre of the bay, but the resort sports some rather ugly older-style block hotels.

However, in the peak of the season it is one of Menorca's most buzzing places and has a good range of restaurants, bars and shops.

Badia de Fornells (Fornells Bay)

There is not much sand around Fornells (*see pp90–91*) but the shallow and protected waters of the Badia de Fornells south of the town offer one of the best watersports environments in Menorca, perfect for windsurfing, paragliding, sailing and kayaking. A number of schools run training courses or offer rental equipment so that, whatever your skill level, you can have fun here. Sea kayakers can head out of the inlet and explore the rocky coastline along the north coast with its numerous caves and coves. The most famous cave, the Cova del Angleses (Cave of the English), a huge cathedral-like space, can be reached by boat trips from the marina at Fornells during summer.

Away from the water, the landscape around the bay is open countryside swept by the cold *tramuntana* wind in winter. There are some excellent walking routes, particularly on the uninhabited eastern peninsula. The highest point, the Mola de Fornells on the eastern flank of the mouth of the inlet, rises to 122m (400ft) and offers views back across the coastal plain.

Camí d'en Kane (The Kane Road)

Menorca's first reliable cross-island road was completed during the governorship of Richard Kane (*see pp66–7*) in the early 18th century. It revolutionised transport and communications on the island. The Camí d'en Kane, with its narrow width and high drystone walls, became obsolete as time passed and transport technology improved, but instead of widening it, the Menorcans built a new, faster and wider road, the ME1, which now takes the bulk of the cross-island traffic, leaving Kane's road for those who want to take a road less travelled.

Recently, the island has started to reclaim its heritage and has invested in a new asphalt surface for the road, making it perfect for cycling and a smoother ride for cars. There is little traffic on the route and you can enjoy the views of *llocs* and farmland.

Camí d'en Kane runs west from 2.5km (1½ miles) north of Maó on the 710

The Camí d'en Kane is now a well-tarmacked single-track road popular with cyclists

The coastline of Cap de Favàritx

Maó/Fornells road to the outskirts of Es Mercadal. It sits just north of the ME1.

Cap de Favàritx

The most surreally beautiful spot on Menorca, Cap de Favàritx is a barren grey slate headland jutting north-eastward into the Mediterranean. The earth has played a wonderful trick here, twisting and folding the sedimentary rock so that the layers lie almost vertical. This dark and foreboding spot is pounded by waves and chiselled by wind, flaking into millions of shards that blanket the surface. Standing sentinel above the spray and flotsam is the Cap de Favàritx lighthouse, to warn ships of the dangerous waters offshore.

In the last couple of decades, marine archaeologists have discovered the remains of a Roman shipwreck off the point, serving as proof of its treacherous reefs and currents. Finds brought up from the seabed here include amphorae and coins that shed light on commerce in Menorca during that era. A range of these is on display in the Museu de Menorca in Maó (*see pp42–5*). Nowadays, Cap de Favàritx forms part of the S'Albufera des Grau Natural Park (*see pp92–5*) and is protected land.

Ermita de Fátima

One of several centres of pilgrimage in Menorca, there has been a chapel on the site of the Ermita de Fátima since the Middle Ages. However, the present

FRENCH VERSUS BRITISH
In 1756 the French besieged Fort St Phillip in the Maó inlet (*see pp54–5*) in the opening days of the Seven Years War. Admiral John Byng was dispatched post-haste to Menorca to sort the situation but dragged his heels, finally meeting the French fleet off Cap de Favàritx. The battle was by all accounts a draw but Byng lost confidence and retreated to Gibraltar, sealing the fate of the British garrison on the island.

He paid for his reticence with his life. On his return to his homeland, he was court-martialled and shot for dereliction of duty. This incident inspired Voltaire to comment in his novel *Candide* that the British needed to shoot an admiral now and then 'in order to encourage the others'.

church was built in the 1950s in a pleasant spot on a small hillock surrounded by countryside, and it is a popular place for locals to get married.
Not open regular hours.
Free admission.

Es Grau

This tiny fishing village is the most laid-back coastal settlement on the island. A photogenic cluster of whitewashed cottages set against glistening azure waters dotted with tiny bobbing boats, its waterfront sports small nets and lobster pots ready for tomorrow's catch. Es Grau has its fair share of visitors but there are few places to stay, so tourism hasn't altered life or the landscape too much. This region is part of the S'Albufera des Grau Natural Park and therefore it is not going to change much in the future either. From

Northern Menorca

CALDERETA DE LLAGOSTA

Every restaurant serving this excellent seafood dish has its own secret recipe, but if you want to make it yourself at home here is a reliable option that will get you an authentic result. You will need a terracotta casserole to cook it in, as nothing else seems to work!

Ingredients for four people:

3 live spiny lobsters of 500g (18oz) each
2 litres (4 pints) of fish broth
4 onions (finely chopped)
5 cloves of garlic (finely chopped)
2 large ripe tomatoes (finely chopped with their juice)
0.5 litre (1 pint) of cava brut (sparkling wine)

Fresh parsley
A drop of Spanish brandy
Toasted dried bread
Pepper
Salt
Olive oil

HOW TO COOK

Tie and cook the lobster in the fish broth for 15 minutes, break into chunks (by hand is best) and set aside. In a large open terracotta casserole, fry the onion in the olive oil. When the onion is soft, add the garlic and tomatoes to obtain a loose paste. Add the fish broth and then the cava and let it simmer for 15 minutes. Add the lobster and some of the parsley, then leave to simmer for an hour with the casserole open till the sauce turns rich and creamy. Stir in the brandy and serve from the casserole with a sprinkle of parsley and toasted bread.

here you can take a boat trip to the Illa d'en Colom (*see pp91–2*); the beaches to the west are unspoilt and uncrowded – reached only on foot. It is also an easy route to the park information centre.

Fornells

Set on the banks of a large lake-like inlet, the smart village of Fornells is a pretty string of whitewashed buildings with painted shutters nestling against a palm-lined waterside, a picture-perfect fishing community with a heavy dollop of tourism dropped into it. It is a popular anchorage for the summer yachting crowd and one of the most visited places on the island for its *caldereta de llagosta*, a mouthwatering lobster stew that is the signature dish of Menorca. Restaurants line the

waterfront and they all serve *caldereta* – certainly the most expensive dish on the menu – and other delicious and fresh seafood dishes like *caldereta de marisco* (assorted seafood stew) at less than half the price.

The village grew up around Fort Sant Antoni, built in the 1600s to protect against the Ottoman threat (*see pp11–12*) but now in ruins. Some 1.5km (1 mile) north of Fornells, at the mouth of the inlet, is a recently renovated Martello tower built by the British in 1798 before they departed Menorca for the last time. The **Torre de Fornells** looks a bit over-restored although it will weather in time. There is a small military museum inside. In the shadow of the tower is a tiny but immaculately kept shrine, the Ermita de Loudres, where the fishermen's wives come to offer prayers for the safe return of their menfolk.

The platjas de Fornells (Fornells beaches) lie to the west of the Fornells peninsula, the best being Cala Tirant, reached by road south of Fornells. This wild beach backed by grass-covered dunes has developed a sandy spit that protects a small marshland filled with birds, fish and reptiles.

Torre de Fornells. www.gfornells.com. Open: Apr & Oct Tue–Sun 9.30am– 3pm; May–Sept Tue–Sat 9.30am–8pm, Sun–Mon 9.30am–3pm. Admission charge (free on Sun).

Illa d'en Colom (Pigeon Island)

Lying just offshore and forming part of the Parc Naturel de S'Albufera des Grau (*see pp92–5*) and easily accessible by boat from Es Grau's little harbour, the Illa d'en Colom is Menorca's largest offshore island. There are several quiet beaches to enjoy on the sheltered western shore. The British built a

The narrow, picturesque streets of Fornells

quarantine station here during their stewardship, which was in use until a new complex was built on the Illa del Llatzeret (*see pp60–61*). The remains make a walk into the interior worthwhile. Watch out for lizards scurrying to and fro in the undergrowth; they are Lilford's wall lizards, a subspecies indigenous to Menorca and predating the arrival of man, but now found only on protected offshore islands.

Parc Naturel de S'Albufera des Grau (S'Albufera des Grau Natural Park)

Menorca's showcase park acts as the core of the UNESCO biosphere reserve, and over an area of just over 5,000 hectares (12,355 acres), covers a whole

Parc Naturel de S'Albufera des Grau (S'Albufera des Grau Natural Park)

gamut of environments and ecosystems that are typical of the Tramuntana region of the island. The park was created in direct response to development plans proposed in the 1970s that would have changed this coast irrevocably. Extreme conservation methods have recently seen the revival of the marram grasses around the dunes bordering Es Grau beach and the return of rare birdlife to the wetlands and marshy shores.

The park ranges across coves and inlets from Punta de sa Galera just east of Es Grau village (*see pp89–90*) to Punta de Mongofra, taking in the coastal waters and the offshore Illes des Porros in the west; inland it stretches up to 3km (2 miles) into the hinterland. The greater area is made up of a hotchpotch of different levels of protection, ranging from 'area of use conditional on conservation' where

The spring-fed lagoon in the natural park

THE MEADOWS OF THE SEA

Menorca is surrounded by hectares of sea-grasses, including Neptune grass and Posidonia. These form vast meadows or prairies, and scientists now know that they have played an invaluable role in maintaining the coastal landscape and seawater.

They produce oxygen and organic materials that allow fish and other marine creatures to breathe and feed.

They stabilise the seabed and attract more sand. They temper the force of the waves, stopping the sand from being washed away.

They offer shelter and protection to several sea species, including sea urchins and starfish, and provide a breeding environment for fish.

farmers and fishermen continue to work within agreed guidelines, to 'strict nature reserve' where there is minimal human influence.

The strictly protected areas encompass the offshore islands – Illa d'en Colom and Illes des Porros, plus two small landlocked sections, Bassa de Morella and Es Prat. There is one strict marine area in the far north, the tiny inlet of s'Estany, which is home to rare marine plants such as the manatee grass.

Much of the park's important vegetation is low-growing, including lentisk shrub and jasmine box. Even lower-growing are the socarrells, the generic name for dwarf shrubs that live

Dramatic cliffs on the north coast

in close proximity to salt water. Some of these can only be found on Menorca. The offshore waters protect acres of Posidonia – an important marine vegetation species (*see box, p93*).

The main area of interest close to the park's visitor centre (just west of Es Grau) is the wetland. The spring-fed freshwater lagoon covers 70 hectares (173 acres) and is the largest in Menorca, offering ideal conditions for waterfowl, including coot and mallard, and a host of seasonal visitors. Underwater species such as eel and striped mullet abound. Wild fauna include the European pine marten and significant populations of Iberian frogs

and toads. There are a couple of lookout points along the footpaths – marked routes of between 20 and 50 minutes' duration – so take binoculars to get the best view of the birdlife.

The geology of the park will interest amateur scientists. The rocks in this region of Menorca are the oldest in the Balearics and include examples from the Carboniferous period (at Cap de Favàritx – *see p89*), the Mesozoic (red ferrous rocks at Es Capell del Ferro) and the Quaternary (fossils at Illa d'en Colom and Mongofra).

The areas of farmland within the boundaries that now protect flora and fauna have become an established part

NATIONAL PARK RULES

- Don't drive off prescribed routes.
- Stay on the prescribed paths, as walking on plants can damage delicate or rare environments.
- No dogs are allowed in the park.
- Don't pick the plants, feed or disturb the animals.
- Respect walls, barriers and access routes, as most of the land in the park is still private property.
- Don't cross the dunes to the beach at Es Grau, as this is a highly fragile environment that is now starting to thrive again.
- Camping overnight and the lighting of fires are forbidden.
- No boats may anchor where Posidonia grows (*see p93*).
- Don't remove slate from Cap de Favàritx (*see p89*).
- Don't fish anywhere along the north coast.

of Menorca's ecosystem due to man's intervention and the traditional farming practices that have shaped the environment through the centuries. Many plants, birds and insects rely on the continuance of these traditional land uses, including the growing of crops like olives and the grazing of cattle.

Much of the land around the access road to Cap de Favàritx is covered under the 'conditional' section and it is interesting to watch the gradual change in vegetation from lush farmland to vegetation more suited to dry conditions, to succulent species that need little water, to no vegetation at all by the time you reach the cape itself.

Centro de Recepción Rodríguez Femenias. Ctra de Maó es Grau 3.5km, Llimpa. Tel: 971 35 63 02. www.mallorcaweb.net/salbufera. Open: summer Wed–Sat 9am–6pm, Sun 9am–3pm; winter Wed–Sun 9am–3pm. Free admission.

Sant Joan des Horts

Founded in the 17th century in the northern shadow of Monte Toro (*see pp109–11*), this tiny church was reconstructed in 1807 in neoclassical style and was one of Menorca's pilgrimage churches. Today it is an evocative ruin surrounded by lush farmland, and the stone rose window on a façade devoid of glass stands stark against the sky.

Son Parc

The sprawling north-coast resort of Son Parc is the site of the island's only golf course (it is 18-hole and has a thriving restaurant popular with English expats) and a single fine sandy beach, both of which are set against fragrant pine forest. The bay has escaped over-development with low-rise apartment blocks and few supporting restaurants and bars, which means the beach rarely gets crowded. It's a long walk down to the beach (past the sewage treatment plant!) from the urban area and there is only one restaurant there. There are some excellent walking routes west to Badia de Fornells or east to the resorts of Arenal d'en Castell, Na Macaret and Addaia.

Drive: Maó to Fornells

This short drive from the capital to the north coast leads you to some of Menorca's most important wildlife habitats. It is an opportunity to do a bit of birdspotting (see pp166–7) or windsurfing before finishing the trip just in time for lunch at one of the fine restaurants in Fornells (see p171).

Time: 3 hours.
Distance: 45km (28 miles).

Leave Maó on the road along the southern flank of the harbour heading west. From a roundabout at the head of the inlet, take the ME7 signposted Fornells. After 1km (²/₃ mile) take the right turn on the ME5 towards Es Grau. After 5km (3 miles) there is a left turn along a country road into the Parc Naturel de S'Albufera des Grau.

1 Parc Naturel de S'Albufera des Grau

The information office for the park (*see pp92–5*) is on the left a few hundred metres down this road. Stop here for information in English. Proceed to the parking area and choose one of the three walking routes around the freshwater lagoon with its prolific birdlife. There are lookouts with views across the water, and panels with pictures of birds you are likely to see. *Return to the main road and turn left. Make your way 1km (²/₃ mile) or so into Es Grau. Leave your car in one of the two car parks just at the edge of the village, as access is limited.*

2 Es Grau

Although there are no major attractions in Es Grau, there is always something going on: fishermen landing their catches, mending nets or repairing boats, and every little whitewashed cottage has some pretty detail to enjoy. You can take a boat to the Illa d'en Colom (*see pp91–2*) to explore this protected island or combine this drive with the walking route on pages 98–9. *Leave Es Grau by the same route you entered and retrace your route back to the junction with the ME7. Turn right here in the direction of Fornells. After 5km (3 miles) a small mound appears on the right with a stone church on the top.*

3 Ermita de Fátima

The Ermita de Fátima is a relatively modern building (*see p89*) but the history of this hermitage dates back centuries. The church is not open regular hours.
From the church, continue towards Fornells. The road leads on through

rolling farmland with Monte Toro up ahead on the horizon. Eventually, 13km (8 miles) from Ermita de Fátima, the ME7 reaches a T-junction. Take a right turn and after 1.5km (1 mile) you will see the Badia de Fornells on your right.

4 Badia de Fornells

The narrow outlet of the bay creates the perfect wind conditions for windsurfing and sailing boats.

Drive on to Fornells. Park at the base of the Torre de Fornells.

5 Torre de Fornells

Fornells Watchtower was built by the British (see p91) during the Napoleonic era. The coastal views are spectacular. Return to Fornells.

6 Fornells

Take a stroll along the palm-shaded promenade and explore the village.

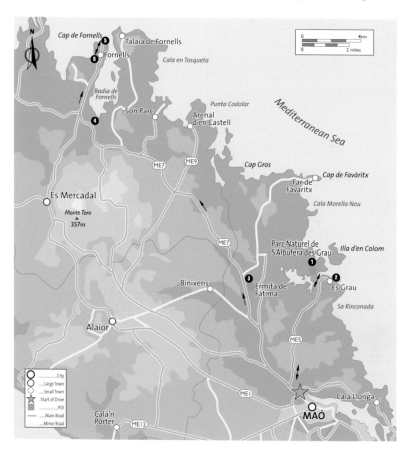

0 ____ 4km
0 ____ 2 miles

Cap de Fornells
Talaia de Fornells
Fornells
Cala en Tosqueta
Badia de Fornells
Son Parc
Punta Codolar
Arenal d'en Castell
Mediterranean Sea
Es Mercadal
Monte Toro 357m
ME7
ME9
Cap Gros
Cap de Favàritx
Far de Favàritx
Cala Morella Nou
ME7
Parc Naturel de S'Albufera des Grau
Illa d'en Colom
Binixens
Ermita de Fátima
Es Grau
Sa Rinconada
Alaior
ME5
Cala Llonga
Cala'n Porter
ME12
MAÓ
ME1

O ____ City
O ____ Large Town
O ____ Small Town
★ ____ Start of Drive
■ ____ POI
— ____ Main Road
— ____ Minor Road

Walk: Es Grau to Sa Torreta

Areas of northern Menorcan countryside are best seen on foot. From this perspective you can appreciate the complexity of the low-growing plant life and myriad insects enjoying the pollen. This route is set in the heart of the Parc Naturel de S'Albufera des Grau (see pp92–5) and combines coastal and inland sections, finishing at Sa Torreta. Take plenty of water, sunblock and a sun hat with you.

Time: 4 hours.
Distance: 10km (6 miles) round trip.

Leave your car in the car park at Es Grau and set off west around the head of the Es Grau beach, taking an old bridal path called Camí de Cavalls, which runs around much of the island. At the far end, the path rises over a low headland, the Roca des Mabres. Keep right until you reach a second smaller bay with a white house at the far end of the strand.

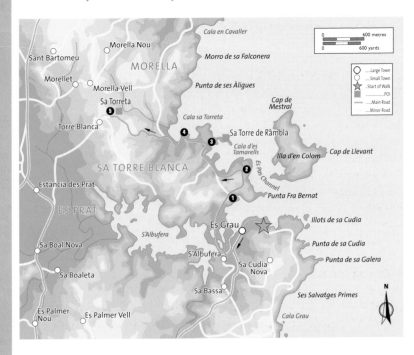

1 The White House

The White House is open as a café in high season and it is your last chance for refreshments. There are great views back across the bay to Es Grau from here.

From just before the White House, a well-worn path heads inland to the left, over the headland. Keep walking towards the Illa d'en Colom, which lies directly ahead across the Es Pas Channel.

2 Illa d'en Colom

Enjoy the views out to the little island (*see pp91–2*) across the bay from the cliff-top path.

From the cliff top, the path swings inland cutting across another headland from where the coastline opens up ahead. Walk down to the bay of Fondejador des Llanes where the route hugs the coast up to the Cala d'es Tamarells.

3 Cala d'es Tamarells

The northwestern tip of the Cala d'es Tamarells, Es Colomar is marked by a ruined Martello tower, Sa Torre de Rambla, built by the British in the 18th century.

Turn left across the headland leaving the tower and coastline on your right. From here there are excellent views inland across the Parc Naturel de S'Albufera des Grau.

4 Cala sa Torreta

The park covers an area of over 5,000ha (12,355 acres); but this view takes in the lake at S'Albufera, the largest freshwater ecosystem on the island.

The majestic *taula* at the Sa Torreta site

The next bay you reach is Cala sa Torreta. Walk halfway across it before turning inland (left) through low alpine shrubland towards another ancient site.

5 Sa Torreta

There are fewer ancient sites in the north of the island than in the south and Sa Torreta is probably the best of these. The site is scattered and rather overgrown but this only adds to the fun and the atmosphere. The huge *taula* (4m/13ft) is probably the most impressive single feature; you will also find a *talaiot*, a threshing floor and several Talayotic houses among the wild olives.

From here the easiest plan is to head back to Es Grau by the route you came, although there is a route leading south past the Sa Torreta lloc (farmhouse), which leads to the northern shores of S'Albufera lake before cutting back to meet the original path at the Cala d'es Tamarells for the return to Es Grau.

Southern Menorca

The south of Menorca, known as the Migjorn, is a vast swathe of sedimentary sandstone laid down in the Miocene period that has been carved by wind and water into a series of small valleys or barrancas *running south to the sea. The pale, rutted ground rock, softened by holm oak, vine and olive groves, offers some of the most evocative landscapes on the island, and is home to some of its prettiest resorts.*

Several *barranca* outlets now play host to tourist developments, from the long-established Cala'n Porter to the more recent Cala Galdana, nestled around cosy fine-sand beaches. Coincidentally, the Migjorn also boasts Menorca's longest beaches – Son Bou and Sant Tomàs.

Even in the 21st century, some of the south coast is beyond the reach of modern vehicles, and getting about on foot brings rewards by the basketload:

tiny coves, long-distance views from cliff tops and remote Talayotic settlements where the only sounds are the humming of cicadas and the scuttling of ground lizards.

North of the *barrancas* lies a string of inland towns comprising Alaior, Es Mercadal and Ferreries, the major economic and administrative centres of the island. Each very different in character, they offer a chance to explore the modern Catalan heart of the island, one step removed from coastal tourism.

Alaior

Ask most Menorcans about Alaior and they will mention Mahón cheese. The town has two famous factories, Coinga and La Payesa, where you can buy direct. But there is more to the town than cheese.

Alaior was given its municipal charter by Jaume II at the start of the 14th century. Since then, it has remained the administrative town for the centre of the island, and the third in line fighting over the role of capital, with Maó and Ciutadella being the first two. It was a centre of learning with a private university in 1439 and this ensured its independence until the 1700s. During the Kane governorship of the early 18th century (*see pp66–7*), land around the town was drained and it became a major fruit-producing area. Later, footwear became an important industry.

The town sits on a medieval plan with a core of narrow alleyways, which creep up- and downhill; it's a great place to explore in the cool of late afternoon. A couple of old windmills rise above the whitewashed cottages but the main architectural attraction is the soft sandstone **Església Santa Eulàlia** (Church of St Eulalia), which dominates the high ground and has been the subject of a recent facelift. Founded in the 14th century but reworked in the late 1600s, the exterior styling is more in keeping with military than religious architecture, with two plain towers flanking the vast, plain Baroque façade. Attention is focused on the exquisite doorway with its fine carved detail, while the interior remains pure Gothic with minimal decorative elements.

The former town hall or Ajuntament building is an excellent example of a Baroque palace, although the entrance patio was added in the 19th century.

A unique building in town is Pati de Sa Lluna, a former Franciscan convent built in the late 17th century that was converted into family homes after the expulsion of the religious order in 1835. The four storeys erected around a central patio have remained unaltered and are usually festooned with family washing while the courtyard, known as Sa Lluna, is a popular setting for the commune's concerts and folk-dancing.

There are interesting little shops strung along the hilly main street of Carrer des Ramal and lots of local bars and cafés, as well as a couple of quality restaurants.

Skyline of the medieval city of Alaior

Just outside the municipality, the pilgrimage site of Sant Llorenc de Binixems holds a procession during the second week of August leading from the church into the town.

Cala'n Porter

One of Menorca's longest-established tourist resorts, Cala'n Porter typifies why the island attracts so many tourists. Set on a narrow, rocky *cala* with a gentle golden beach and limpid azure water, it is stunningly attractive. The *barrancas* inland offer typical lush landscapes to be explored on foot.

The resort accommodation sits on the cliff tops above the beach – a steep but short climb (or you can take the mini-train that chugs remorselessly around the resort). There is a good selection of restaurants, bars and clubs to keep all ages happy, although the styling of some of the buildings is beginning to look a little dated and the roads could do with some repair.

Travel through the resort centre to reach one of the major attractions in

Menorca, **Cova d'en Xoroi** (the Caves of Xoroi), a labyrinth of natural caverns cut high in the cliff face overlooking the sea. After exploring the inner recesses, look out from the cave mouths to the pounding waters below. The caves have been transformed into a club with bar, café, state-of-the-art music system and world-class DJs. It is packed with sightseers by day and transforms into the island's most famous club on summer nights.

Cova d'en Xoroi. Tel: 971 37 72 36. www.covadenxoroi.com.
Nightclub open: mid-May–mid-Sept 9pm–dawn; bar all day from 10.30am. Admission charge includes a drink during the day.

Cala Galdana (also known as San Galdana, Santa Galdana and Cala de Santa Galdana)

Set at the base of the deepest *barranca* on the south coast, Cala Galdana appears like a holidaymaker's paradise at the end of the long access road. A crescent-shaped beach surrounded by high cliffs and palm trees, it is sometimes known as the 'queen of the coves' for its sheer beauty. The *cala* forms the end of the Barranc d'Algender, which cuts deep into the hinterland. The mouth of the ravine forms a popular marina for small fishing and tour boats that offer sightseeing trips along the coast as well as a few yachts.

Accommodation is a mixture of high- and low-rise, with the huge Hotel

RTM Audax to the west of the bay only marginally detracting from the panorama. There are eateries and bars lining the beach and dotted all around the resort, although nightlife is pretty low-key.

The Barranc d'Algender is the largest in the Migjorn. It is a mini-ravine biting 11km (7 miles) into the island, and it is the only one with a permanent watercourse running through it. The *barranca* offers a whole range of natural environments – from fully marine saltwater to brackish to freshwater – as you travel inland. The animals and plants reflect the level of salinity in the groundwater with wild holm oak and olive, the only elm trees on the island and pines in the upper reaches, and vast swathes of reed beds just inland from the resort. This is an excellent place for amateur ornithologists and animal lovers; there are burgeoning populations of red kites and other birds of prey, as well as a profusion of insects, including iridescent dragonflies. The cliffs close to Cala Galdana and inland offer an excellent environment for butterflies and are a popular nesting site for migratory swallows, which visit in their hundreds of thousands in summer.

The rocky coastline on either side of the resort shelter some exquisite beaches that can be reached on foot for a day of walking, swimming and sunbathing on stretches that are less busy than the main resort. About 1km (²/₃ mile) to the east is Cala Mitjana, where swimmers can get inside the limestone caves. There are no beach facilities here, so take water and

Cala Galdana is one of the most popular beaches on the island

sunblock. The same distance in the opposite direction, you will find Cala Macarella, where there is a beach bar and several caves cut into the cliffs. Just over the headland is the tiny hideaway of Cala Macarelleta.

Cales Coves

One of the wildest and most beautiful *calas* on the south coast, this narrow, curving rocky inlet filled with crystal-clear turquoise water and hiding a tiny pearl of a beach is the yachtsmen's favourite Menorcan anchorage. Over land it can only be reached by a signposted 2km (1¼-mile)-long rough track from Son Vitamina.

Two ravines converge here and the water has sculpted some amazing shapes into the limestone. Numerous pre-Talayotic cave dwellings and a necropolis have been sculpted from the natural caves, which were used as a place of pilgrimage until Roman times. Artefacts

found during excavations here are on display in the Museu de Menorca in Maó (*see pp42–5*).

The caves became a popular hippy hangout in the 1970s. Although the 'summer of love' lasted longer here than in many places, it didn't survive into the new millennium. Now the cave-dwellers have been evicted and the site is on the protected list, although you'll find a few enterprising backpackers reappearing in the summer.
Open access. Free admission.

Cova des Coloms (Cave of the Pigeons)

Set in the heart of *barranca* countryside, the Cave of the Pigeons is one of the biggest inland caverns on the island. It has been given the nickname 'the Cathedral' for its height and width. Excavations here have revealed that the cave served as a centre of cult worship for the Talayotic peoples that lived in the surrounding countryside.

The cave is often used as an impromptu rave venue by locals or as a refuge by disrespectful backpackers, which accounts for the soot and burn stains around the walls.
Cova des Coloms. From Es Migjorn Gran, drive along the road to San Adeodato beach. From there follow a path along the beach and off to the right until you reach Barranc de Binigaus Vell. Go up the valley on the left side; the path leads to the cave. Open access. Free admission.

THE LEGEND OF XOROI

The caves at Cala'n Porter are named after the main character in one of Menorca's best-known legends. Xoroi ('one ear') was a Moorish pirate who was shipwrecked on the island and hid out in these remote caves. After a while he felt the need for some female companionship, so he kidnapped a young virgin girl from her family home in Alaior.

He kept the girl prisoner for many years and she bore him several children, but eventually Xoroi was discovered when he left telltale footprints during a rare winter snowstorm. When cornered he chose suicide and threw himself from the cliffs with his sons.

The crystal-clear turquoise waters of Cales Coves

The old windmill in Es Mercadal

Es Mercadal

This attractive town forms the natural crossroads of the island, a junction between roads leading north, south, east and west. It was the natural place to stop for refreshment at a time when travel was undertaken at a more leisurely pace, and is still known for its classy gastronomy, the abundance of shops selling sweet pastries and the flamboyant displays of horsemanship during its dazzling July fiesta.

The name 'Mercadal' originates from the fact that the town was once the major market town of the island where locals came to sell their fruit, vegetables and traditional wares, and a market is still held every Tuesday and Saturday afternoon. The proximity of Monte Toro (*see pp109–11*), with its massive statue of Jesus and convent, just a couple of kilometres above the town also made it a natural settling point. Remains from Talayotic and Roman times are evidence that the area has a long history.

The town owes its present status to Jaume II, who founded a parish here in the early 1400s. A group of settlers arrived from mainland Spain and the building of Fort Agueda just a few kilometres away guaranteed economic viability.

The licence to hold a market in medieval times gave the town its name. It was the administrative centre for much of the western interior of Menorca until the mid-19th century. Es Mercadal lost control of Es Migjorn Gran as recently as 1989 as a result of an island reshuffle.

Església Sant Martí, built in simple Baroque style and whitewashed, is the dominant building as you approach the town, but the main feature as you drive past on the main road is the old windmill, now converted into a popular restaurant called Es Molí d'es Racó. Shop on Carrer Nou (the main street) for *ensaïmades* (sweet pastries) and munch tapas on Plaça Constitució, the busy main square.

The town benefited most directly from the massive *aljub* or public cistern built by Governor Kane (*see pp66–7*) in the 18th century to alleviate chronic water shortages. Locals still arrive with buckets and other containers to take free water when the gates are open.
Aljub des Mercadal. Open: Sat 10am–1pm. Free admission.

Es Migjorn Gran

Menorca's youngest municipality, Es Migjorn Gran, sits on the route down to Sant Tomàs, slightly off the main ME1 from Maó to Ciutadella, and perhaps this has helped the town retain its cosy, village feel. The town was founded in the late 18th century as San Cristóbel, but took its new name, meaning 'the big south', when it gained political independence from Es Mercadal in 1989. There is no special attraction that stands out here, though the simple church of Sant Cristòfol straddles the Baroque and neoclassical styles, and there are a couple of good traditional

Huge development has changed the face of Ferreries

restaurants to be found among the simple whitewashed family homes in the shady streets.

Local hero Francesc Camps I Mercadal (also known as Francesc d'Albranca) is remembered for his collections of folkloric tales, songs and dances that have kept Menorcan culture alive. Today his legacy lives on as the town is one of the most active in these traditional arts, contributing musicians and dance troupes to many festivals and celebrations around the island (*see pp26–7*).

Farinara S'Arangí

You can't miss this large complex set on the side of the ME1 between Alaior (*see pp101–2*) and Es Mercadal (*see p107*). This old mill is one of a new breed of tourism enterprises – part-museum, part-shopping centre, it offers a stop

that caters to the whole family with a small American Indian themed park for children plus a bar and restaurant. The mill dates from 1905. All the threshing and grinding machinery are still in situ and have been restored. The warehouses, with their original wooden floors and ceilings, are now the retail area selling souvenirs that run the whole gamut – although there's more mass-produced stuff than handcrafted goods. *Carretera Maó–Ciutadella, Es Mercadal. Tel: 971 15 43 08. Museum open: Tue, Fri & Sat 9am–2pm. Shopping: daily 9am–8pm. Admission charge for museum.*

Ferreries

The highest town in Menorca, Ferreries was founded by Jaume II. It is thought that the name derives from the number of blacksmiths working here – an ironworks is *ferreria* in Catalan. The outskirts of Ferreries have developed beyond all recognition in the last 20 years because of recent huge development that focused on the footwear and furniture industries and brought prosperity to the town. However, there are pockets of the old town left – if you head to the higher part of the town you will see some handsome 18th-century houses, neatly whitewashed with brightly painted shutters, which line the narrow jumble of sun-baked backstreets. The main square – Plaça de l'Església – is one of the prettiest corners of town flanked by the small whitewashed church of San Bartomeu and a couple of tapas bars.

Centre de la Natura (Museum of Nature) has a small exhibition devoted to environmental issues, but most people visit for the huge open-air market held every Tuesday and Friday in the modern main square, Plaça d'Espanya. A number of concerts are also held there during the summer, as well as a craft market each Saturday. *Centre de la Natura de Menorca. Carrer Mallorca 2. Tel: 971 37 45 05. www.gobmenorca.com/cnatura. Open: late May–Oct Tue–Sat 10.30am–1pm & 5.30–8.30pm, Sun 10am–1pm. Opening hours vary in winter; check with the museum. Admission charge.*

Monte Toro

Menorca's highest point has exerted a strong spiritual influence on the island throughout its known history. Though by no means a true mountain at a height of only 357m (1,171ft), it nonetheless offers spectacular

Jesus watches over his flock from the top of Monte Toro

View of Es Mercadal from Monte Toro

views across the island, and, on early spring or late autumn days, rises above the dewy morning mist that blankets the lowlands.

The access road heads out of Es Mercadal and ends in a series of steep switchback turns leading up to the car park. Here, amid a rash of communications antennae that keep Menorca in touch with the world, is the holiest site on the island: a Catholic sanctuary built to house a statue of the Virgin Mary (the Verge del Toro, patron of the island), said to be imbued with miraculous powers. A simple Gothic building was initially erected to house the statue, and the Franciscans expanded this into a monastery complex. The place got an ornate Baroque makeover in the 17th century, but was defiled soon after the Franco regime took power in the 1930s,

although the statue was saved. Mary stands holding the infant Jesus with a trusty bull (*toro*) at her feet at the centre of a mock-Baroque altar, the result of repairs carried out in the 1940s. A community of Franciscan nuns now cares for the complex.

Crowning the peak is a large statue depicting Christ with his arms outstretched and now almost lost among the antennae. The figure stands on an earlier edifice raised to commemorate the Menorcans who fell during wars with Morocco in the 1920s; it was added by the bishop of the island in 1939 to commemorate the end of the Civil War. Monte Toro welcomes a steady stream of pilgrims through the year (as well as people simply coming to admire the amazing views) but truly comes alive during the Festa de la Verge del Toro (Festival of the Virgin of the

Bull) on 8 May when, following Mass at the church, the congregation heads down the hill for a lively knees-up in Es Mercadal.

What's in a name?

Menorcans will tell you that the mountain was named Monte Toro because a wild bull (*toro*) with silver horns led a group of monks to a cave on the peak to discover the statue of the Virgin. More probably, the name comes from the Arabic *al-tor* meaning 'high ground', and the Spanish created the legend to cover the original root of the name as it was devised by their old adversaries.

Navetes de Rafal Rubi

Twin *navetes* are rare, so it is good to see these siblings standing in a farmer's field close to the main cross-island road just outside Maó. A well-worn path leads to these communal burial structures resembling upturned boats, one in a better state of preservation than the other. The style and building quality indicate that these belong to the pre-Talayotic era, making them some of the oldest on the island and a contrast to the Naveta des Tudons (*see pp128–9*), which is much finer in quality and later in date. *ME1, Km 6.6. Open access.*

Sant Tomàs

The 3km (2-mile)-long beach at Sant Tomàs (in fact, two beaches, Sant Tomàs and Sant Adeodato, although visitors may not notice the tiny rocky outcrop that separates the two) was undoubtedly the reason for the resort being founded here. The beach is

The tombs at Navetes de Rafal Rubi

Southern Menorca

Remains of the palaeo-Christian church at Son Bou

backed by dunes and dominated by the white edifice of the Sant Tomàs Hotel. The tourist infrastructure has developed fast and this is a good place for watersports enthusiasts – you can also hire sunbeds, parasols and pedalos here, and there are a couple of decent beach bars. If you are a novice or non-swimmer, be aware that there are strong undercurrents offshore. The resort is a good base from which to explore the southern *barrancas*: several marked footpaths lead out along the coastline or inland to numerous caves, including the impressive Cova des Coloms. The best route is along the Barranc de Binigaus Vell.

Son Bou

The longest beach on the island at 4km (2½ miles), Son Bou is a wide golden stretch that seems to go on forever, and is a total contrast to the cosy *calas* of 'n Porter (*see p102*) or 'n Blanes (*see p120*). The duneland backing the fine sand is also unusual for the south of the island. In the centre of the bay, the freshwater reed beds, Es Prat, caused by the natural damming of a river outlet, are the largest of their type in Menorca, and a rich environment for birds, reptiles, butterflies and insects – including mosquitoes. The reed beds are currently under a conservation order. Son Bou is one of the youngest resorts on the island, with a proliferation of low-rise villas and apartment blocks climbing the hillside north of the coastal plain. These are generally in good taste (although areas of the Centro Comercial could do with a lick of paint) but the same can't be said of the high-rise twin monoliths **Sol Milanos Pingüinos** Hotel, which dominates the east end of the bay. Still, Son Bou offers a good range of tourist services, from restaurants and bars to watersports facilities, and a few classy shops like Timberland are starting to appear.

The bay at Son Bou also houses some important ancient sites. The remains of the largest palaeo-Christian basilica in Menorca sit on the eastern flank of the beach. The ground plan with its three naves is clearly visible, although there's not much else to see. Soon after its discovery in 1951, archaeologists also found traces of a small surrounding settlement, but these haven't been preserved. Behind the church are more ancient carved caves, part of a Talayotic necropolis. A few of these are used as bohemian holiday homes complete with painted shutters and sun terraces.

Just as at Sant Tomàs just around the coast, the sea at Son Bou has strong undercurrents. Look out for the warning flags before you swim. *Palaeo-Christian basilica. Walled site, open access.*

Son Mercer de Baix

One of the oldest ancient settlements yet excavated on the island, Son Mercer de Baix is quite difficult to get to, so a visit offers the chance to explore a site without too many 21st-century distractions.

The countryside here is spectacular. Set among two lush *barrancas* are the remains of several Stone Age houses and *navetas*, including the Cova d'es Moro (Moor's Cave), a large house with a roof supported by three stone pillars. This single building is now classed as a Menorcan National Monument.

Close to the farm of Son Mercer de Baix, on the eastern slopes of Barranc d'en Fideu, 3km (2 miles) south of Ferreries. Follow the treacherous narrow track carefully and proceed on foot for the last 600m (660yds). Open access. Free admission.

Talaiots de Sant Agusti Vell

Close to the Cova des Coloms (*see p104*) is the early ancient site of Sant Agusti Vell, set at the peak of a typical *barranca*. There are the remains of several houses and a collection of *sitjots* (storage chambers) carved out of rock. When in use, these would have been

Talayotic remains at Torre d'en Galmés

A cove on the southern coast

covered with stone slabs. The finest remains on the site are two high *talaiots* (*see p83*), one of which has a chamber you can climb into. The main interior structures are the two stone pillars supporting the upper structure. The village was inhabited from the pre-Talayotic to the Roman era, and finds include artefacts of Phoenician origin. *Access on foot to the west of the ME18 Es Migjorn Gran to Sant Tomàs road. Open access (the route is not good). Free admission.*

Torre d'en Galmés

The largest Talayotic town in Menorca, Torre d'en Galmés sits on a gentle hill with views in all directions. The lower part of the settlement comprises numerous stone homes, many still with their impressive pillars, although the stone roofs they supported are no longer set atop them. Around them a handful of *sitjots* (or storage chambers) is carved into the base rock. Climbing

up through the village, more unexcavated buildings come into view. The village has three *talaiots* and a *taula* set within its enclosure, although the ceremonial slab has been dislodged from the top.

The settlement finds cover the same eras as the Sant Agusti Vell site (*see above*) but archaeologists have also found medieval remains, suggesting that a part of the village was occupied well after this time. The finest piece discovered is the ancient Egyptian brass statue of the High Priest Imhotep that is now on display in the Museu de Menorca (*see pp42–5*) in Maó.

The necropolis site of Ses Roques Llises lies 300m (330yds) beyond the village. Dating back to the pre-Talayotic period, it comprises a rectangular chamber lined with large flagstones and, close to this, a large ancient structure of five chambers and a walled patio with the separate name of Na Comerma de sa Garita.

Signposted on a single-track road off the Son Bou road. Open: daily 10am–8pm. Admission charge.

Torralba d'en Salort

One of the most easily comprehensible of the island's many ancient sites, Torralba d'en Salort has been thoroughly excavated since the 1970s, and is the village that has added most to the growing academic understanding of pre-Talayotic and Talayotic cultures in Menorca. The site is made up of several houses inhabited throughout prehistory, a central *talaiot*, the tallest *taula* on the island, a quarry, threshing area and sections of an outer wall – suggesting that some of the sites were protected by fortifications. At some time during the intervening centuries, the site was cut by a country lane but the route is now diverted around the site.

Carbon tests show that the site was established around 1400 BC, with the Talayotic houses dating from about 1300 BC. When the *taula* area was excavated, archaeologists discovered many cult items, including terracotta figures of a Punic deity and a small ceremonial bronze bull that links these ancient people with other bull-worshipping cults around the Mediterranean basin. These finds are all dated to the 2nd and 1st centuries BC, and are on display in the Museu de Menorca in Maó.

More mundane items were discovered in the houses: the bones of numerous ovicaprids (ancient forms of sheep and goat), and wheat and barley seeds that indicated the inhabitants' regular diet.

There are no *navetes* at the site but it does include a series of funerary hypogea or artificial caves to contain bodies, carved in the rock.

4km (2¹/₂ miles) southeast of Alaior on the Cala'n Porter road. Open: Apr–Sept daily 10am–8pm (closed first Sat of the month); Oct–Mar hours vary. Admission charge Apr–Sept.

Taula and other ruins at Torralba d'en Salort

Menorcan cheese

Cheese has long been a speciality of Menorca

One of the staples of the farming industry, Menorcan cheese (*queso*) has developed into an art form. The Moors sang its praises and Menorcans were exporting it across the Mediterranean as early as the 13th century.

In 1985, Menorcan cheese-makers were granted a 'denomination of origin' mark – which means that only cheese produced on the island under the strict guidelines of the regulatory authority may be given the label 'Mahón-Menorca'. Each Denominación de Origen Protegida (D.O.P.) cheese is quality-checked and has a numbered label to protect its quality.

Before the advent of modern technology, cheese was made and cured on the farm (*lloc*). Curing involved turning the cheese regularly and rubbing the rind with a blend of oils and spices – each farm had its own secret recipe – that would impart a particular flavour. Today, many of the cheeses are made in factories but quality is still paramount.

WHAT TO TASTE

Today's product is made and air-cured or matured following long-established traditions, from fine-quality cow's milk. It is sold in four main categories:

Young

These are cheeses that have been matured for between 21 and 60 days. The product has a soft, supple and elastic texture, and a pale yellow colour. The flavour is just a little sharp.

Semi-cured

As the cheese matures further, it takes on a lighter colour with a brownish or orange slightly wrinkled rind and a firmer texture. It has a characteristic smell and a tangier flavour. A cheese is classed as semi-cured when it is between two and five months old.

Cured

With further maturing the cheese hardens, the texture becomes more brittle and crumbly, and the taste stronger. It is classed as 'cured' when it has been maturing for over five months.

Aged

With a rind that resembles old leather and flesh the colour of parchment, these are cheeses that have matured for well over a year or longer. The flavour has strength and complexity, and a long aftertaste. It is excellent when accompanied by a fortified wine.

Names to look for

The following brands have been recognised by the Menorcan Cheese Council (for more details consult *www.quesomahonmenorca.com* – in Spanish only): Binibeca, Coinga, Dalrit, H. De FCO Quintana, Hort de Sant Patrici, Marqués, Mercadal, La Payesa, Sa Casanova, Subaida and Torralba.

WHERE TO TRY IT

You can taste Menorcan cheese at market stalls, in shops or try it in one of the island's recipes: in a delicious four-cheese soup with some of each style incorporated into the recipe, or in cheese ice cream – which tastes much better than it sounds – served crème brûlée-style with a crispy sweet coating.

The town of Alaior (*see pp101–2*) is a centre of commercial cheese production with two factories – Coinga (*Carrer d'Es Mercadal*) and La Payesa (*Carrer d'Es Banyer 64*).

Menorcan cheese-makers can use the 'denomination of origin' mark on their produce

Western Menorca

The sunset coast of Menorca is anchored on Ciutadella, a city of sandstone mansions, the religious heart of the island and its prettiest port. The old town is enjoyable at any time of day but a warm glow becomes palpable as evening descends and the streets come alive with locals after the long afternoon siesta.

Just a couple of kilometres north of the town is the island's largest tourist agglomeration – four tiny but picture-perfect *calas* collectively known as Cala'n Forcat, which have grown into a small town full of budget hotels, apartment blocks and eateries. In the evenings it is a good place to sample genuine fish and chips and a refreshing drink.

Cala'n Bosch on the south coast has more sand and fewer hotels, plus a marina that is the perfect spot for a tourist-dominated *paseo* and a waterfront dinner.

These two resorts offer over 90 per cent of the accommodation in the west but it is easy to escape the crowds by going to the *calas* of the west, called *platjes verges* (virgin beaches) by the Menorcans for their unspoilt natural beauty. Cala'n Turqueta east of Cala'n Bosch is considered the most beautiful on the island, but there are many more whose golden sands and azure waters backed by limestone cliffs are just waiting to be discovered.

The landscape around Ciutadella epitomises the contrast between the Migjorn and the Tramuntana (*see p6*). To the south you will find date palms and citrus groves, while to the north the eye sees nothing but arid desert with kilometres of drystone walls, hundreds of *barraques* (pyramid-shaped drystone huts used as sheep or cattle pens by the farmers) and the odd farmhouse.

Cala d'Algaiarens

Lying east of Cala Morell, the twin beaches of d'Algaiarens are two of the north coast's most exquisite horseshoe bays of fine golden sand, backed by tall pines. They are impossible to reach by public transport and the landowner limits the number of cars travelling across his land to the bays. The trip makes for a great cycle ride and the quiet beaches are certainly worth it. *Intersection of the Cala Morell road. 3.5km (2¼ miles) to the beach. Access charge for vehicles.*

Cala'n Bosch (Cala en Bosc)

Cala'n Bosch successfully combines beach resort with lively marina, and is one of Menorca's enduring family favourites. The town beach is pretty but on the small side. The wider Platja Son Xoriguer is within walking distance to the east and has been incorporated into a growing upmarket resort area. The marina is a lovely place for an evening stroll, lined with buzzing restaurants and bars. You can take a day trip from here or rent boats, and head out to explore the coast.

On the outskirts of Cala'n Bosch you will find an alternative to the sticky sand and salty water of the beach at **Aquarock**, with huge pools, slides, Jacuzzi and a children's play area, which also incorporates **KartingRock**, a karting track with single or double karts.
Aquarock: Off Via de Circumval Lagó. Tel: 971 38 78 22.
www.aquarock-menorca.com

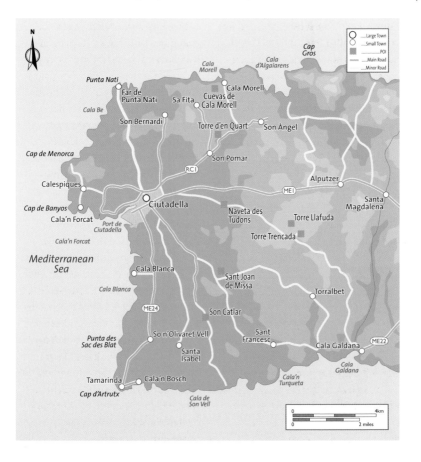

Open: May–Oct daily 10.30am–6pm.
KartingRock: Off Via de Circumval Lagó.
Tel: 971 38 78 22. Open: May–Oct daily
10.30am–10.30pm in peak season.
Admission charge.

Cala'n Forcat

Several tourist developments merged
along the coast in the area just north
of Ciutadella, around a series of
picturesque narrow *calas*. The once
individual resorts of Cala'n Blanes,
Cala'n Bruch, Cala'n Forcat and Cales
Piques have merged into a mega-resort
centred on the Los Delphines complex,
where most of the bars, cafés,
restaurants and clubs are found. In high
season, the little coves are filled by
visitors sunning themselves on the
beach or the bathing platforms that
cling to the cliffsides. There is nothing

The whitewashed walls of Cala Morell

sophisticated here, just pure family fun
with big-screen matches in the football
season accompanied by an English or
German pint.

The resort boasts a water park that
has slides, chutes, freshwater pools and
a bar restaurant. The large hotel and
apartment complexes have discos in
peak season for night owls.
Aquacenter: Avinguda de los Delfines,
Cala'n Blanes. Tel: 971 38 82 51;
restaurant tel: 971 38 87 05.
www.aquacenter-menorca.com.
Open: May–Aug daily 10.30am–6.30pm;
Sept & Oct Tue, Thur & Sun
10.30am–6.30pm. Admission charge.

Cala Morell

Cala Morell has a stark and alluring
beauty. A barren rocky inlet sheltering
a postage stamp-sized golden beach, it
makes an incredible anchorage for
yachters. The only vegetation around
is hundreds of cultivated palms and
colourful bougainvillea, softening the
lines of the upmarket, whitewashed
villas that tumble down the cliffs. The
panorama is one of the most dramatic
in Menorca.

Cala Morell is an artificial oasis in
one of the least populated parts of the
island and one could be forgiven for
thinking that only modern man has the
wherewithal to survive here. In fact the
cliffs around the resort have one of the
highest densities of rock-cut ancient
caves in Europe, and around 1000 BC
the bay was buzzing with the activities
of the Talayotic people.

The **Cuevas de Cala Morell** bring home the sophistication of these people. Expansive chambers interlink to create the interiors similar to a modern studio apartment, with carved wall niches and windows. There are over 15 caves in total, some used as dwellings, and others as storage areas and ossuaries, and they were in use from pre-Talayotic times to the end of the Roman era.

On the approach to town, look out for the **Torre d'en Quart**, a sturdy medieval tower built to protect against pirate attack and now incorporated into a typical *lloc* complex. There is a tiny stony beach and a couple of restaurants; Bar a l'Estiu has pride of place on the track leading down to the beach and has great views of the odd rock formations to the west of the inlet. *Cuevas de Cala Morell. Open access. Admission charge.*

Cap d'Artrutx

Menorca's southwesternmost corner is a rugged, rocky spot marked by a mid-19th-century lighthouse that was an important guide for ships (*see p137*). There are incredible sunsets here and clear views of the island of Mallorca less than 40km (25 miles) away, but otherwise not much to do or see.

The tower close by, Talaia d'Artrutx, dates from 1588 and was one of a series built in the wake of violent Ottoman attacks. A string of towers around the coast acted as an early warning system. In times of danger a warning fire would be lit at one tower, which could be seen by the next tower down the coast, which would in turn light a fire, and so on, until the whole island was on alert.

Ciutadella

Menorca's old capital is its most beautiful city. When the British took executive power away from Ciutadella in 1722, they inadvertently did its citizens a favour, preserving for posterity the patrician palaces and religious institutions. Once a walled citadel, the town is a compact district encompassed by tree-lined avenues and the sea. The port is the perfect

The strange rock formations at Cala Morell

place for an evening aperitif and alfresco dinner.

Founded by the Carthaginians, the town was the only major settlement on the island at the time of the Moorish takeover (some theologians contend that it was already a bishopric), and was the natural site for their capital, Medina Minurka, which sat on the site of the present Plaça de la Catedral. The town was given the name Ciutadella when the Christians retook the island and it remained the capital with power concentrated in the hands of a few influential families even when sovereignty passed through the hands of many other European powers.

In 1558 the city was destroyed by Ottoman forces, allied with France. Well over half of the population was forcibly taken to Istanbul to be sold in the slave markets. Only a hefty ransom paid by the remaining islanders could secure their release.

Houses in the old town of Ciutadella

The city was reinforced in the wake of the attacks but that didn't make it any more enticing to the British, who coveted the massive harbour at Maó for strategic reasons. When the islands finally became and remained Spanish in 1802, Maó was proclaimed as capital but religious power stayed at Ciutadella – and the patrician families stayed put in the town.

With the growing population bursting through the city walls, they were demolished in 1860. In the following decades the city thrived as a centre of the shoe industry. It suffered during the Spanish Civil War in 1936 after the garrison declared loyalty to Franco, while the rest of the island remained staunchly for the Republic. Many of the churches were ransacked in violent retribution.

Today, the city is a wonderful throwback to a bygone era with fine architecture on every corner. Although we have listed the major attractions here, wandering through the narrow streets is the best way to appreciate the grace and beauty of the whole.

Bastió de Sa Font and the Museu Municipal de Ciutadella (Ciutadella Municipal Museum)

The only remaining element of the vast 17th-century city wall, Bastió de Sa Font stands strong and proud at the head of the Ciutadella inlet. After it lost its strategic value as a fortification, it became a factory producing acetylene gas and then was part of the municipal waterworks before being renovated as the town museum.

The expansive lower vaults display an interesting collection of artefacts from ancient sites in the western part of the island, including excavated skeletons and ritual objects. They also house models of several megalithic settlements.

Plaça de Sa Font. Tel: 971 38 02 97. www.ciutadella.org/museu. Open: Oct–Apr Tue–Sat 10am–2pm; May–Sept daily 10am–2pm & 6–9pm. Admission charge (free on Wed).

Catedral de Santa Maria

Before the Moorish takeover of the island, an 8th-century parish church of Santa Maria stood on this spot.

The main entrance to Catedral de Santa Maria

The present building was founded on the site of the main mosque of the Medina Minurka (the bell tower is part of the Islamic complex) in the first days after Alfonso III retook the islands in 1287. This basic Gothic core, with its vast single nave, still sits at the heart of today's cathedral.

Badly damaged in the Ottoman attacks of 1558, the flying buttresses were reinforced against possible further attack, giving the exterior the peculiar box shape it has today. It was renovated in the style of the day with the addition of several Baroque side chapels, the finest of which is La Capilla de las Animas (Chapel of the Souls).

The original 14th-century entranceway, the Port de la Llum, is still in situ with the coats of arms of Aragon and of the city incorporated into the decoration. Today's main door – a grand portico – on the western façade was part of an early 19th-century makeover that was started soon after the church was elevated to the status of cathedral in 1795.

Plaça de la Catedral. Open: Mon–Sat 10am–2pm.

Es Port (the harbour)

The port sits in the shadow of the town, and the narrow *cala* at Ciutadella gives it a much cosier feel than the waterfront in Maó. It is lined with old whitewashed cottages appearing to grow out of the cliffs and houses hordes of restaurants and bars, while yachts and tour boats bob at the nearby quayside.

This is a great place to stroll and is particularly atmospheric in the evenings. You can reach the port via a wide set of steps – the biaxada de Capllonc – that are filled with stalls selling crafts and souvenirs in the late afternoon, or the Moll del Costa that weaves its way down from behind the Ajuntament in Plaça d'Es Born. From the north bank of the cove there are great views back across the port and up to the town above.

Head up the creek inland to Es Pla de Sant Joan, where the cliffs house ancient caves and warehouses, some converted into restaurants and trendy nightclubs. The upper terraces on the square offer some of the best views of the Festa de Sant Joan (*see p129*) when jousting contests and displays of horsemanship are held here on 23–24 June.

Església del Roser (Roser Church)

The finest example of Churrigueresque architecture (*see p25*) in Menorca, this tiny church was built at the beginning of the 18th century and is little altered from the original. The exterior decoration reveals a wealth of ornate tracery. Now deconsecrated, the interior hosts exhibitions of contemporary art. *Carrer del Roser. Open: Mon–Sat 10am–1pm & 5–8pm. Free admission.*

Mercat (Market)

The meat and charcuterie market with neat tiled stalls was created in 1868 by

Façade of the cathedral

adapting the cloisters of the Augustinian monastery complex behind it. A separate 19th-century tiled pavilion houses a small fish market (the *pescaderia*). This is a bustling district where locals gather for a gossip and coffee before heading home for lunch. *Plaça de la Llibertat. Open: Tue–Sat 8am–1pm.*

Museu Diocesà de Menorca (Diocesan Museum of Menorca)

Hidden behind another monolithic Baroque façade are the remains of the 17th-century convent of St Augustine, which now host the Diocesan Museum. As with Maó's Museu de Menorca (*see pp42–5*), the architectural elements of this building are as interesting as the museum artefacts. The Mediterranean-style Baroque cloisters make a fine statement.

The galleries have some surprising inclusions, such as an archaeological gallery that has the personal collection of Bishop Mercader, including bronze statues dating from the 5th century BC. Other exhibits include paintings by the 20th-century Catalan artist Pere Daura, who was known for his landscapes. The more expected objects include an array of liturgical and religious artefacts, including several in gold and silver, dating from the 17th to the 20th centuries.

The Augustine convent church of El Socors is now a music venue, with concerts at 11.30am from Tuesday to Thursday in June and September.

Boats moored at Es Port, Ciutadella

Carrer del Seminari 7. Tel: 971 48 12 97. Open: Tue–Sat 10.30am–1.30pm. Admission charge.

Pedreres de S'Hostal

The sandstone of the Migjorn has been used as building material for millennia. Its warm hue enhances the Talayotic, Gothic, Baroque and Modernist buildings across the island. Its structure made it easy to shape, giving us the fine carved portals of churches such as Santa Eulàlia at Alaior (*see p101*) and the Catedral de Santa Maria in Ciutadella (*see p123*). There are working quarries of sandstone across the island even now, but most of the old ones have been abandoned or put to use as communal rubbish dumps, making them a detraction from the landscape rather than an element in Menorca's socio-economic heritage.

Lithica has changed all that. This non-profit organisation aims to

Ciutadella's harbourfront is lined with restaurants and bars

rehabilitate the sites of the old quarries, and to educate Menorcans and visitors about the important role played by these 'holes in the ground'.

The quarry workings at Ciutadella were worked for over 200 years before they were closed in 1994. The cuttings demonstrate two different means of extraction: the 19th-century hammer-and-chisel approach leaving a maze of block-work towers and indents behind; and the 20th-century method involving huge circular saws that could cut deeper vertically into the stone, leaving vast clean faces.

At S'Hostal, the complex has been planted with native and tropical plants. Olives, oranges and almonds offer shade, and there are several water features to enjoy. It is a wonderful place to wander around, with interesting views into the quarry and a whole host of butterflies, insects and birds.

The cathedral-like dimensions of the 20th-century quarry are put to good use as it doubles as a concert venue on summer evenings.

Camí Vell (1km/ ²/₃ mile east of town).
Tel: 971 48 15 78. www.lithica.es.
Open: summer daily 9.30am–sunset,
Jul–Aug Sun 9.30am–3pm & 5–9pm;
winter Sat–Sun 10am–sunset, Mon–Fri
10am–1pm. Admission charge.

Plaça d'es Born

The finest town square in Menorca, Plaça d'es Born is an open space, home to trees, cafés and the town's biweekly market (*Fri & Sat am*). From the northern flank there is a viewing point – the *mirador* – down to the port below. Menorca's natural sandstone has been used to exceptional effect here to erect several impressive buildings around the periphery. These give the appearance of having been here for centuries but in fact they are mostly 19th-century. At the heart of the square is an obelisk commemorating the 1558 attack on the city by Ottoman forces.

The eye-catching **Ajuntament** (once the town hall, now the police headquarters) has traces of old Moorish architecture with its arches and fringe of date palms. The building sits on the site of a Roman temple. Teatre des Born on the northern façade was built on the site of the old British barracks building in 1873, and was the centre for the arts in western Menorca; at the time of writing it was closed.

On the eastern flank are two exceptional 19th-century palaces that together form an architectural whole. Both have impressive neoclassical façades featuring three-arched loggias on the first floor. The Palau de Torre Saura is the larger of the two, with twin towers linked by a single-storey entrance topped by a family coat of arms. Next door is the Palau de Salort, set at an angle to the square, its main façade overlooking Carrer Major des Born. Both palaces are still in private hands but the period interior décor and furniture of Palau de Salort is on view to the public during restricted hours.

Església de Sant Francesc at the southwestern corner of the square was once part of a larger convent complex. It was destroyed in the 1558 attack,

The Ajuntament in Plaça d'es Born, Ciutadella

and restored and augmented in the following centuries. The façade was the final addition in the 19th century.
Palau de Salort. Open: May–Oct Mon–Sat 10am–2pm. Admission charge.

Ses Voltes (The Arches)

At one section of the main shopping alleyway running through the Plaça de la Cathedral to meet up with the Camí de Maó are Ses Voltes, two sets of arcaded Gothic-style buildings. They have vaulted porticos with houses above and shops set underneath the wide arches at ground level. Ses Voltes forms a chic shopping area and borders on to Plaça Nova, lined with cafés.

The mouth of the harbour

The mouth of the Ciutadella inlet is a pleasant walk of around 1km (²⁄₃ mile) from the port. The narrow and rocky channel makes it clear why the Royal Navy wouldn't have wanted to run a base from here. The regular ferry

Ciutadella harbour

between here and Mallorca seems to manage pretty well, though, and it is fun to watch its immense bulk sliding between the inlet's walls, reminiscent of tankers traversing the Suez Canal.

On the north side of the inlet is the lighthouse of Punta na Mari; on the south is the small but perfectly formed **Castell de Sant Nicolau**, built at the end of the 16th century to defend the port and town. The tower was restored in the 1980s and is now used to house temporary exhibitions.
Castell de Sant Nicolau. Plaça Admiral Farragut. Tel: 971 38 10 50.
Open: Tue–Sun 10am–1pm & 6–8pm. Free admission.

Naveta des Tudons

The finest single ancient building in Menorca and one of the most complete ancient ossuaries in Europe (claims have been made that it is the oldest roofed

---

A MENORCAN IN AMERICA

David Glasgow Farragut was the son of a Ciutadellan who emigrated to the United States. He fought in the Civil War and was head of the force that took New Orleans. Eventually he reached the rank of Admiral – the first in the American Navy. When he visited Ciutadella in 1867 he was welcomed as a celebrity and it is said that the crowd was so dense that Farragut's carriage couldn't finish its journey and he had to walk the final section, with well-wishers tugging at him. There's a bust dedicated to Farragut in the square in front of Castell Sant Nicolau (*see above*).

building on the continent), the Naveta des Tudons marks a high point in the building techniques and burial rituals of the pre-Talayotic and Talayotic peoples. During earlier phases, the bones of the dead were interred in caves or carved hypogea. The *naveta* represented a sophisticated development, a custom-built and monolithic tomb where ancestors and their treasured possessions could rest in peace.

In use between 1200 and 750 BC, the Naveta des Tudons was a large (14m × 6m/46ft × 20ft) communal tomb with two internal chambers. It was fully excavated in the 1950s, when the remains of over 100 individuals were found with grave goods including bronze bracelets, bone buttons and clay pots.

5km (3 miles) east of Ciutadella. Tel: 902 92 90 15. Open: Sun & Mon 9am–3pm, Tue–Sat 9am–8pm. Admission charge.

Punta Nati

The lighthouse at Punta Nati was built on its bleak and arid headland at the beginning of the 20th century with money donated by the French after one of their cross-Mediterranean passenger ships ran aground on the rocks, killing or injuring over 200 people. There are several walking trails along the coastline from here and it offers exceptional sunset views.

This route makes for a great cycling trip from Ciutadella or from the Cala'n Forcat resorts because it is mostly along single-track lanes through flat farmland; you will need to carry your own refreshments, though. If you are driving, practise your three-point turns for the lane outside the lighthouse!

FESTA DE SANT JOAN

The Festival of St John is Menorca's most important religious and cultural celebration. The two-day festivities were begun in the 14th century as a show of prestige by the city's patrician families. Over the centuries, it developed into a display of horsemanship. Even in the present day, responsibility for organisation of the celebration is passed from one family to another every two years. The year's *Caixer Senyor* manages the show and its complicated rituals.

The Sunday before the 24th, *S'Homo d'es Bé* (*Man of the Lamb*), a representation of John the Baptist clad in fleece and carrying a lamb, is paraded through the town by a party of horsemen.

On the 23rd, a cavalcade starts the festivities at 2pm to the accompaniment of the *jaleo* (traditional music played on a flute) and a host of medieval flags and costumes. The black horses or *bot*, on their hind legs with front legs high in the air, trot around Plaça d'es Born – this is Menorcan dressage at its very best. At 7.30pm there is a Mass at Sant Joan de Missa (*see p132*) in the countryside outside the town.

On the morning of the 24th there are jousting trials in Plaça Sant Joan (open ground at the head of the Ciutadella inlet), and then a Mass at the cathedral. At 6pm the master of the *festa* is invited to come and watch the climax of the jousts when only the most skilled horsemen appear. When the victors are declared, there is a final cavalcade that wends its way to the Church of Santa Clara. A spectacular fireworks display ends the day.

Walk: The sights of Ciutadella

Much of the old district of Ciutadella is off-limits to traffic so it is very pleasant to stroll around. This route is short but packed with attractions; look out for old palaces, ornate churches and chic shops along the way. Stop off at any point to put your feet up in a bar or café – you'll find plenty. The best time to follow this walk is late in the afternoon when all Ciutadella appears for the ritual paseo *around town.*

Time: 2½ hours.
Distance: 2.5km (1½ miles).

Start at the Plaça d'es Born. If you have arrived by car the square offers parking except on market days (Fri & Sat am). Otherwise, park on Avinguda de Jaume I.

1 Plaça d'es Born

Stroll around Plaça des Born enjoying the façades of the 19th-century palaces and the Ajuntament with its Moorish details (*see p127*). The obelisk commemorates the 1558 attack on the city by Ottoman forces.
Leave the square by Carrer Major des Born, which leads between the two decorative palaces (see p127) on the east side of the square.

2 Carrer Major des Born

The lower, vaulted storeys of the buildings of Carrer Major des Born now house a range of shops selling souvenirs, shoes and all sorts of quality Menorcan foodstuffs.

After a few minutes, you will enter Plaça de la Catedral.

3 Catedral de Santa Maria

On the left is the Catedral de Santa Maria, with its Gothic core embellished by Baroque and 19th-century additions (*see p123*).
Exit the cathedral and turn left to leave the square. On your left you will find the first section of Ses Voltes.

4 Ses Voltes

The arcades of Ses Voltes run for 300m (330yds) in two sections. The vaults house a variety of shops from souvenir emporia to high-class boutiques.
Where Ses Voltes meets Plaça Nova head down Camí de Maó to Plaça ses Palmeres. Turn right and right again down Carrer d'Alaior, then turn left into Carrer La Palma and right into Plaça de la Llibertat.

5 Mercat (Market)

Ciutadella's daily food market takes place here, with a row of tiled kiosks selling fresh vegetables. A separate glass building houses the fish market (*pescaderia*). The market is busiest in the mornings and closes at about 1pm.

From the market, continue down Castell Rupit and turn first right. The Museu Diocesà de Menorca is in front of you.

6 Museu Diocesà de Menorca

The former convent is an excellent example of Baroque architecture. The adjoining Església El Socors holds organ concerts in summer (*see p155*).

With the museum on your right-hand side, turn left down Carrer del Santíssim and first right along Carrer del Roser back into Plaça de la Catedral. With the cathedral on your right, take the first left and then the first right down Carrer Forn to Pere Capilonc. Turn left here and head down the steps to Es Port.

7 Es Port

Stroll past the yachts moored at the quayside and look up to your left for views of the rock face and buildings above, floodlit in the evening.

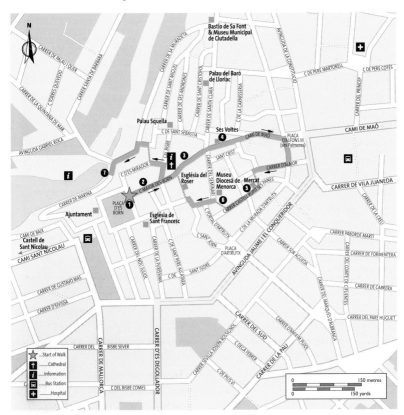

The Talayotic burial chamber of Naveta des Tudons

Sant Joan de Missa

Founded in the first days after the re-establishment of Christianity on the island at the end of the 13th century, the original Gothic *ermita* has undergone many extensions and renovations, including battlements

WITHIN THESE WALLS

The prehistoric site at **Son Catlar** in the countryside southeast of Ciutadella is the only one to have retained its immense defensive wall. It extends for almost a kilometre (¹/₂ mile) and, within the compound, you can explore five *talaiots* and other scattered remains.
8km (5 miles) southeast of Ciutadella.
Open: daily 10am–sunset. Admission charge in summer.

added in the 1630s – the whitewash does a fair job in bringing the disparate elements into a coherent whole.

The chapel, also known locally as Sant Joan Gran, is the centre of attention during the Festa de Sant Joan (*see p129*) when a colourful procession wends its way from Ciutadella to attend Mass.
4km (2¹/₂ miles) southeast of Ciutadella. Not open regular hours. Free admission.

Torre Llafuda

The *talaiot* of this ancient village is believed to be the largest in Menorca.

A small *taula* and a cave plus short sections of a cyclopean wall and stone passageways are still visible. The settlement was one of the most important in the region during Roman times and was inhabited until the end of the Moorish era.

Just off the ME1 at Km 37. Open access. Free admission.

Torre Trencada

This ancient site has yet to be fully excavated and contrasts with the village at Torralba d'en Salort (*see p115*), which is well signposted and mapped. It's a 10-minute walk along a dusty track through woodland and scrub to this magical place. Those who enjoy history will love clambering among the remains of ancient stone houses. The main attraction is the *taula*, thought to be still in its original configuration, as the ancients intended, though the enclosure has been lost. The site is believed to have been inhabited until the Middle Ages.

7km (4¹/₂ miles) east of Ciutadella on the Camí Vell (Maó–Ciutadella old road). Open: daily Apr–mid-Nov 8am–9pm; mid-Nov–Mar 8am–6pm. Free admission.

The lighthouse in Punta Nati was built at the beginning of the last century

Two drives: Across the spine of Menorca and Menorcan lighthouses

Menorca is a compact island and you can easily get from east to west in just over an hour. The first drive takes you meandering along the main ME1, which links several fascinating towns. The route finishes at Ciutadella, where you can take a reviving drink on the harbour side at Es Port (see pp123–4) and wander the streets of the old town.

The second tour has lighthouses as its theme, but it also leads you through some of the island's most splendid landscapes and most remote corners.

DRIVE 1: ACROSS THE SPINE OF MENORCA

Distance: 56km (35 miles).
Time: 6 hours.

Leave Maó travelling west along the waterfront until you reach a roundabout. Take route ME7 towards Fornells. After 2.5km (1½ miles), turn left on the Camí d'en Kane. See purple route on map.

1 Camí d'en Kane

The Camí d'en Kane (*see p87*) is the cross-island road built under the auspices of Richard Kane, the first British Governor of Menorca, in the early 19th century. The route is rather narrow and winding, with high dry-stone walls leading through some wonderful rolling countryside. It runs just north of the ME1.

Follow Camí d'en Kane until you reach the outskirts of Alaior after 10km (6 miles). There is a left turn at the town cemetery, which leads into the town.

2 Alaior

Alaior is famous for its cheese (*see pp116–17*). Visit the factories of Coinga and La Payesa to buy supplies and stroll in the lanes of the old town, which are lined with majestic town houses. The newly cleaned Església Santa Eulàlia has a fine Baroque façade. If you are there at lunchtime, head for Transparent in Plaça Ramal for tapas and a cold beer. *From Alaior, pick up the main ME1 by following directions for Ciutadella (this main route bypasses the town to the south but is well signposted from the centre). Continue west until you reach the Farinara S'Arangí on the right after 7km (4 miles).*

3 Farinara S'Arangí

This mill complex (*see p108*), built in 1905, now houses a museum, shopping mall, bar and restaurant – even a small park for children. Opening hours are somewhat erratic, especially in winter. *From the mill, continue west on the ME1 for 1km (²/₃ mile). On the outskirts of Es Mercadal follow signs off to the right for Monte Toro and climb the steep winding road to the summit.*

4 Monte Toro

Monte Toro is Menorca's highest point and there are almost 360° views from the peak. The huge statue of Christ was added after the Civil War in the late 1930s but there has been a convent on the site for several hundred years (*see pp109–11*). This is the home of the iconic statue of the Virgin with the Bull, the patron saint of the island. Explore the convent (there is a café there) and admire the views across the island. You can see Badia de Fornells (*see pp86–7*) to the north and, on a clear day, Mallorca to the west.

Descend the hill again, turn left at the bottom and follow the signs into Es Mercadal.

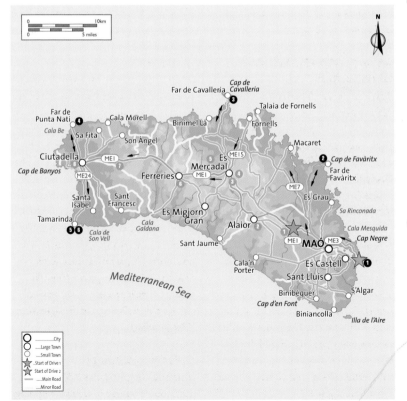

5 Es Mercadal

Founded in the 14th century, Es Mercadal is home to lots of bakeries selling pastries and a few good restaurants. Wander down Carrer Nou and Plaça Constitució and explore the backstreets of this endearing little town. A vast communal *aljub* or water cistern was built on the outskirts of town during Kane's governorship (*see pp66–7*).
Return to the ME1 and continue west to Ferreries, reached after 8km (5 miles).

6 Ferreries

Ferreries is a centre of traditional music and dance. Performances take place throughout the summer on Plaça d'Espanya, where there is a thriving craft market on Saturday in the summer. Plaça de l'Església is flanked by the small, whitewashed church of San Bartomeu and the town hall sprouts brightly coloured flags.
Follow the signs back to the ME1 and continue west. After about 10km (6 miles), look for signs on the left to the car park for the Naveta des Tudons.

7 Naveta des Tudons

One of the finest ancient monuments in Europe, the Naveta des Tudons is situated 300m (330yds) away from the road down a dusty but well-used track. Shaped like an upturned boat, it houses a communal ossuary chamber.
From the naveta, *turn left on the ME1 – it is only 4km (2¹/₂ miles) to your destination, the city of Ciutadella.*

8 Ciutadella

The attractions at Ciutadella can fill a whole day (*see pp121–8*) and strolling through the shady streets of the old town is the perfect end to a long day. Window-shop around Ses Voltes (*see p128*) and then round off the day at one of the many restaurants along the waterfront at Es Port.

DRIVE 2: MENORCAN LIGHTHOUSES
Distance: 125km (78 miles).
Time: 8 hours.

Leave Maó by the road on the southern flank of the inlet west to a roundabout. Take the right turn signposted La Mola (the ME3), which leads along the north of the inlet down the La Mola peninsula to Fortalesa Isabel II (see pp58–60). From the car park here walk north to Punta de S'Espero. See orange route on map.

1 Punta de S'Espero

The lighthouse at Punta de S'Espero marks Menorca's most easterly spot.
Retrace your steps to the roundabout and take the right turn signposted Fornells (the ME7). Continue along this route for 8km (5 miles) before taking a right turn marked Cap de Favàritx.

2 Cap de Favàritx

The lighthouse at Cap de Favàritx is the only splash of colour on the wind-blasted peninsula, part of the Parc Naturel de S'Albufera des Grau.

Retrace your journey back to the ME7 and turn right following signs for Fornells. At the T-junction with the ME15 (12.5km/8 miles), turn right and then almost immediately left, following the country road past Ses Casetes Velles and on for 4km (2½ miles) before turning right for Cap de Cavalleria. After 8km (5 miles) you reach the tip.

3 Cap de Cavalleria

The 90m (295ft) cliffs at Cap de Cavalleria mark the northernmost point on mainland Menorca. There is a little ecomuseum close by with a shady café under pine trees.

Make your way back to the ME15 and turn right to Es Mercadal, where you meet the main cross-island route, the ME1. Follow signs to Ciutadella and after 24km (15 miles) on the outskirts of the town, turn right on the ring road signposted Cala Blanes. Follow this narrow road until you reach a right turning for Punta Nati.

4 Punta Nati

The single-track road leading up to Punta Nati is surrounded by barren country dotted with huge stone sheep-pens. Birds of prey circle over the arid-looking farmland and it is extremely difficult to turn a car around outside the gates of the lighthouse.

Return to Ciutadella and turn left – following signs for Maó would be easiest at this point. When you reach the ring road, follow signs for Cala'n Bosch. The ME24 leads 9km (5½ miles) to the

The lighthouse at Cap de Favàritx

outskirts of the resort, from where Cap d'Artrutx is signposted just a couple of hundred metres ahead.

5 Cap d'Artrutx

The Cap d'Artrutx lighthouse was built in 1868 on this rocky southwesterly outcrop, with splendid views to Mallorca on clear days and some sensational sunsets.

Return to the main road into Cala n'Bosch and park opposite the marina.

6 Cala n'Bosch

Venture into the marina for a cold beer or tapas in a waterfront café.

Two drives: Across the spine of Menorca and Menorcan lighthouses

Getting away from it all

Menorca is a small island and gets packed with tourists in summer but it is still amazingly easy to leave the crowds behind. A maze of dirt tracks that complement the network of smooth, asphalted roads leads to secret coves, whitewashed llocs, remote ancient sites and windswept cliffs and promontories.

The island offers even greater rewards to those who are comfortable on bicycles or with donning walking boots. From this perspective you will really be able to appreciate the small details – like lichens on the stone walls or tiny flowers growing close to the ground on rocky outcrops. You will also be able to take in the birdsong and the distant music of sheep bells. You will find herds of sheep massed in the scant shade of oleaster and holm oak trees, especially during hot and dry summer days.

Cap de Cavalleria

Cap de Cavalleria is Menorca's northernmost point, a narrow finger of land that lies far north of the busy resorts. Located to the west of Fornells, it can be reached by a minor although perfectly good road through arid landscapes with rocky bays, such as the Cova des Vell Mari, where there are few sandy stretches.

Although it looks barren, this part of the island was well populated in ancient times and is extremely rich in archaeological remains – so much so that it has been declared an 'area of special interest' by the authorities. The Romans built a city at Sanitja, the sheltered inlet on the western flank, which is currently being excavated. The exciting discoveries here are revealing the rich culture of the cape in the early first millennium. The ongoing work should give us much more information in the decade to come.

The inlet has a little port that is a popular yachting anchorage in summer, and home to just a scattering of tiny fishing boats out of season. On the western tip of the cape there is a ruined Martello tower built by the British in 1798.

At the tip of the cape, reached through a couple of gates (close them after you have gone through), sits the oldest lighthouse on the island. There are some surprising cliffscapes pounded by the Mediterranean with caves that were carved during the Spanish Civil War.

Troglodyte houses in the cliffs behind Son Bou

The lighthouse at Punta Nati

The farm at Cavalleria, 4km
(2½ miles) south of the lighthouse, has
opened an ecomuseum with finds from
the site plus information about the
surrounding environment. There's also
a shady café and a shop.

At the base of the cape to the west is
Platja de Cavalleria, the best beach in
this area and a good place to cool off
after your exploration. Better beaches
lie further to the west.
*Ecomuseu de Cap de Cavalleria,
Camí de Sa Cavalleria, Fornells.
Tel: 971 35 99 99.
www.ecomuseodecavalleria.com.
Open: Apr–Jun & Oct daily 10am–7pm;*
*Jul–Sept daily 10am–8.30pm.
Admission charge.*

Mola de Fornells

To the east of Fornells (*see pp90–91*)
and its bay, the Badia de Fornells (*see
pp86–7*), is the peninsula of Mola de
Fornells. This area offers one of the
easiest ways to enjoy being in the
countryside without heading too far
from a good bar and restaurant.

Most of the cape is easy walking
country, lying less than 40m (130ft)
above sea level. The vegetation is
mostly low-growing here (since the
tramuntana sweeps across the land
throughout the winter), so you can get
excellent views over the landscape and
across to Fornells west across the bay.
The highest point on the peninsula, on
the eastern flank of the mouth of the
narrow inlet, rises to 122m (400ft). It
affords breathtaking views east to the
windswept grey slate of Cap de Favàritx
(*see p89*) and, to the west, Cap de
Cavalleria.

FONERS

In Roman times the Balearic Islands were
noted for their *foners* (slingshot throwers)
who could launch single rocks or other
projectiles with great accuracy and force over
long distances. *Foners* were considered the
snipers of their day and were often sent in at
the start of a battle to shock and disorient the
enemy. Many of them were mercenaries who
sold their services to the highest bidder.
Others made a career in the Roman army and
travelled across the empire from the Levant
to the British Isles.

The arid scenery of Punta Nati

The footpaths lead to several coastal caves along the eastern flank, including the immense Cova dels Anglesos (Cave of the English), a huge cathedral-like space that can also be reached by boat from Fornells during the summer (*Windsurf Fornells; tel: 971 37 64 00; www.windfornells.com*).

Punta Nati environs

The route to Punta Nati (*see p129*) is one of a decreasing number of traditional Menorcan country lanes. Flanked by high drystone walls and only one-and-a-half cars wide, it cuts across the arid plains northeast of Ciutadella. Sections of it have been upgraded to allow for easier access, particularly for bicycles.

The area is extraordinarily beautiful; the sepia-tone landscape of sand-coloured rocks and golden dry grasses is alleviated by the thousands of sheep (if you can't see them you can hear the constant jingling of the bells round their necks) and scores of *barraques* (stone sheep-pens) that rise metres above the ground. These are incredible feats of engineering for their simple task (to protect the flocks from the winter winds and the summer heat), and many of them have been built in the last few years to a traditional design.

A stone sheep-pen in Punta Nati

Eventually, you reach the point at Punta Nati, a desolate place where the rocks plunge headlong into the ocean. There is no parking area here and the lane ends up as a narrow dead-end, but a footpath leads down past the side of the lighthouse (which is not open to the public) to the cliff edge.

From here you can walk along the cliff tops east to the three dramatic inlets of Cala'n Pous, Cala es Morts and Codolar de Torre Nova, where you can watch gulls swooping across the water. The route eventually leads across rough terrain east to Cala Morell after around 5km (3 miles); you'll be glad to find a couple of bars and cafés here to assuage your thirst, but take drinking water with you on the hike.

The *calas* of the southwest

East of Cala'n Bosch (*see pp119–20*) and west of Cala Galdana (*see pp102–4*) lie some of the most beautiful natural *calas* on the island – tiny rocky inlets, some with rug-sized patches of sand at their head and others with wider stretches of crescent-shaped strands.

A coastal path runs the 10km (6 miles) or so between the two resorts, making for an excellent day's hike (although sections of the route are steep). Public transport between the two is not convenient, with stops at Ferreries and again at Ciutadella.

Some of the best beaches on the island can only be reached down lanes or tracks if you have your own transport. The most famous of these is Cala'n Turqueta, considered the most beautiful in Menorca for its diminutive size, fine white sand and backing of pines. The road from Sant Joan de Missa (*see p132*) leads south towards the beach and you have to drive through a farm gate to reach the parking area (parking charge). From here you can pick up sections of the footpath along to Cala Macarella to the east (around 3km/2 miles) or climb the peak of Talia d'Artrutx (83m/272ft).

Further east are two contrasting beaches: the tiny pearl of Cala des Talader (just west of Talia d'Artrutx) and the neighbouring Arenal de Son Saura, a long stretch of west-facing sand backed by extensive sand dunes that gets sunlight late into the day. Behind Son Saura beach is a large reed bed and marshland, which offers ideal conditions for waterbirds, reptiles and insects, particularly large dragonflies and butterflies; nature lovers can spend hours relaxing here. Take a pair of binoculars.

The tiny, secluded beach at Cala'n Turqueta

These beaches are most easily reached from an intersection off the Ciutadella-Cala'n Bosch road at So n'Olivar Vell, which leads to Torre Saura; you may be required to park the car at the farm there (parking charge) and walk the final 2km (1¼ miles).

The northwest coast

Between Cala Morell and Cap de Cavalleria is a stretch of coastline with little vehicular access. The land here is dotted with small farmsteads but there are no towns and villages – just a maze of country lanes and compacted dirt tracks with few road signs. This is way off the tour-group itinerary but makes ideal walking country if you carry a picnic lunch and water. The western beach of Cala Algaiarens and the

THE CAMÍ DE CAVALLS

Although British Governor Kane built the first cross-country road during his tenure in the early 18th century, travel around the island remained difficult. Most locals used boats and the sea was their highway.

When the French took over the island, they created a bridle path all the way around the coastline. This allowed them to set up a warning system in case of attack, whereby riders could gallop to the next guard station to warn of danger. Sections of the Camí de Cavalls (literally 'horse road') were used until Franco's time, but many remote sections fell into disuse after they were created.

Long-term plans are nearly finished to reinstate the Camí for leisure use. You can already enjoy sections from Es Grau (see pp89–90) to Cap de Favàritx (see p89) and long sections along the south coast, perfect for a hack, a gentle amble or a day's cycling.

BE PREPARED

Whatever time of year you head out, it is wise to carry a supply of water in the car or with you when you walk. Many of Menorca's beaches have summer bars where you can get a drink and snacks in high season, but the more remote beaches don't. A picnic or a supply of snacks is a good idea, especially if you are travelling with children.

eastern Platja de Binimel-La are both excellent, but the more you enter the hinterland, the more the coastline turns rocky.

Castell de Santa Àgueda, a couple of kilometres inland from the beach at Binimel La, is certainly worth a visit, although the walk to the remains takes about an hour. This is Menorca's second-highest peak, and a strategic lookout point over the north coast. The castle was built by the Moors on Roman foundations. Roman governors spent their summers here because the air was cooler, and it was here the Arabs retreated to during Alfonso's campaign in 1287. The fort was used by the Christian conquerors, who built a small church that today lies in ruins overgrown by foliage; however, the paved route to the summit is almost totally intact.

Castell de Santa Àgueda. Turn right off the ME1 road going west from Ferreries, signposted Santa Teresa. Open access. Free admission.

The wild southwest

The country lanes of the southwestern corner of Menorca lead to historical sites such as Sant Joan de Missa (*see p132*) and Son Catlar (*see box, p132*). The Artrutx area is a landscape where you can lose yourself among remote farmsteads and ancient remains. There is an excellent cross-country walk from Sant Joan de Missa to the tiny bay at Cala Macarella (*see p104*), where there is a beach bar in summer, then up through Barranc de Santa Anna, and around Puig de Son Tica, the highest point in the area at a monumental 92m (300ft), before returning to Sant Joan de Missa. You couldn't feel further away from civilisation, even though it is less than 30 minutes from Ciutadella.

The quiet dock at Sanitja near Cap de Cavalleria

Getting away from it all

Shopping

For such a tiny island, Menorca has been home to several different craft industries, so it is possible to buy unusual artefacts that you won't find anywhere else.

WHAT TO BUY

Ceramics

Spain is famous for its ceramics and Menorca has fine examples of fired terracotta bowls, pots and jugs to grace your kitchen. Some locals swear you need one of these bowls to make *caldereta de llagosta* (*see p90*) correctly. The prices are very reasonable, but you'll have to carry them as hand luggage or wrap them well in the hold.

Eco-clothing

T-shirts have become standard souvenirs worldwide but Menorca has turned its back on the mass-produced and imported. **Ecòlogica de Menorca** (*www.ecologicademenorca.com*) started off making T-shirts using good-quality cotton, natural dyes and a fine range of muted colours and patterns. They have now added other garments to their list, including sweatshirts and baseball caps, which are sold in boutiques across the island.

Lladro

Lladro porcelain is one of Spain's most famous brands and a collector's dream, with thousands of examples in the catalogue and an ever-changing number of designs in their recognisable pale blues and greys.

Although it is not manufactured on Menorca, Lladro can be bought in a number of stores. **Castillo Menorca** (*Carretera General, Km 35, Ciutadella; tel: 971 38 04 24; www.castillomenorca. com; open: daily 10am–10pm*) has one of the finest collections in the whole of Spain, with pieces priced from around €50 to over €20,000.

Leather goods

Menorca has a long history of fine work in leather and the tradition carries on today with a thriving shoe industry (*see pp150–51*). The leather is wonderfully soft, and many shoes sold with Italian labels are actually produced in Menorca. Shop around and you can pick up some real bargains. Anything by Looky, Patricia, Torres, Pons Quintana or Jaime Mascaró is likely to be good quality. All of these brands have their own shops in Maó and Ciutadella; there is also a massive Jaime Mascaró factory outlet on the outskirts of Ferreries.

Poligon Industrial (*on the main road just outside Ferreries; tel: 971 37 45 00; open: Mon–Fri 9.30am– 8pm, Sat 9.30am–1.30pm & 4.30– 8pm*) produce high-fashion shoes and clothing for the top end of the market.

The mass-produced leather belts, shoes and 'designer' handbags you see in the markets of Maó and Ciutadella are not usually made in Menorca; they are more often imported from Africa or the Far East; they are mass-produced and not good quality.

Food and drink

Xoriguer gin in its distinctive ceramic bottles and other liqueurs have been made on the island since the 18th century (*see pp172–3*). Or you could treat yourself to some of Menorca's famous Mahón cheese (*see pp116–17*), or cured ham and chorizo (all prepacked for travelling).

Stall selling antiques in Plaça de s'Esplanada, Maó

WHERE TO SHOP
Markets

The Menorcan market, as in many other parts of Spain, has a long tradition. It used to bring families into town from the surrounding countryside once a week to sell their produce, buy some provisions and catch up with the latest comings and goings on the island. Today, it continues to be a colourful affair, though the old knife-grinder may be out of business and many of the wares are aimed at tourists, certainly in the summer. Markets start early, often around 8am, and by 2pm the stall-holders are packing up their goods.

Market days

Alaior: *Carrer Pare Huguet, Thur.*
Ciutadella: *Plaça d'es Born, Fri & Sat; produce market, Plaça de la Llibertat, daily.*
Es Castell: *Plaça de s'Esplanada, Mon & Wed.*
Es Mercadal: *Plaça Pare Camps, Sun.*
Es Migjorn Gran: *Plaça de l'Església, Wed.*
Ferreries: *Plaça d'Espanya, Tue & Fri; craft market, Sat in summer.*
Fornells: *Carrer del Mar, Thur.*
Maó: *Plaça de s'Esplanada, Tue & Sat; fresh produce market, Claustre del Carme, Mon–Sat.*
Punta Prima: *Passeig Marítim, Mon, Wed, Sat & Sun.*
Sant Lluís: *Plaça de la Creu, Mon & Wed.*

Shops

For the best shopping, head to the major towns of Maó and Ciutadella,

---

CERÁMICAS LORA

Produces traditional ceramics using ancient Menorcan techniques. Items include beautifully hand-painted dishes, traditional earthenware flasks for farmers, clogs and contemporary pottery designs. The shop and workshop shares space with S'Alambic at Moll de Ponent 33–36, Port de Maó (*tel: 971 35 03 03; www.ceramicaslora.com*).

---

whose streets have a mixture of high-quality and budget options. The major resorts such as Cala'n Bosch cater to beach-loving visitors, and offer blow-up sunbeds, snorkels, flippers and paraphernalia, plus postcards and sunblock. Check out some of the shops below for good-quality souvenirs.

Shops are usually closed for siesta between 1pm and 5pm, and many stay closed on Sundays (in tourist resorts, they may be open throughout the day and on Sundays).

Ciutadella

Charanga Lovely kiddies' clothes in bright colours and tomboy styles. They come at a price, however!
Carrer de Maó 4. Tel: 971 38 05 85.
Davant Linen clothes, Ecòlogica de Menorca T-shirts (*see p146*) and Panama hats to protect hot heads from the sun.
Plaça de la Catedral 7. Tel: 971 38 58 89. www.davant-menorca.com

Es Mercadal

Centre Artesanal de Menorca Great for gifts, this crafts centre sells a wide range

of décor items, including photo frames, lamps, modern interpretations of traditional pottery designs, and colourful and unusual ceramics.
Recinte Firal des Mercadal. Tel: 971 15 44 36.

Galeria del Sol This contemporary gallery has an increasing reputation for exhibiting work by renowned international and Menorcan artists.
Carrer d'es Sol. Tel: 971 37 51 25.

Es Migjorn Gran

Galería de Acualeras Owned by the British watercolourist Graham Byfield, this gallery has exhibitions of his work and that of other local artists.
Carrer Sant Llorenç 12. Tel: 971 37 03 64.

Ferreries

Hort de Sant Patrici Watch the speciality Queso de Mahón being made by traditional methods on the premises and taste before you buy. It's off the rural road from Ciutadella to Torre Trencada (*see p133*).

Camí Ruma-Sant Patrici. Tel: 971 37 37 02. www.santpatrici.com

Maó

S'Alambic There are several souvenir shops around Maó harbour but this has an excellent range of eco-clothing and the ubiquitous Menorcan sandals (*abarcas*). It shares retail space with Cerámicas Lora (*see box opposite*).
Moll de Ponent 33–36, Port de Maó. Tel: 971 35 07 07.

Delicatessen Can Pota Expensive Menorcan olive oils, gins and *turron* (a honey-based confection) to take home with you.
Portal de Mar 11. Tel: 971 36 23 63.

Fortalesa La Mola Branded souvenirs from candles and pencils to mugs and T-shirts, as well as a massive selection of military reading.
Tel: 971 36 40 40. www.fortalesalamola.com

Moraschi Souffle 1957 Superb-quality Italian-made shoes and bags.
Carrer Alaior 8. Tel: 971 36 25 76.

Rubber boats for sale in Cala Galdana

The Menorcan shoe industry

Tanning was an important industry throughout the Balearics during the era of the Moors, but the demand for footwear really took off in the late 19th century. Within a couple of decades, leather footwear was the mainstay of the Menorcan economy and a third of the population was employed in the industry.

The first factories were founded at Ciutadella, but were soon established in the inland towns as well. It was not long before the *zapata a la mahonesa* or 'shoe of Mahon', then made of dark leather decorated with a silver buckle, was considered the height of fashion in the ready markets of France and England.

During the 20th century, mass-production and imports from the Far East hit the island hard. Cheaper and inferior-quality products flooded the European markets and many Menorcan factories, with their high labour overheads, went out of business.

However, those that survived are thriving to this day. They have done this by coming full circle and concentrating on the aspect of the industry that won them customers 100 years ago – quality. They have made sure that they are positioned in the upmarket sector of the industry, making shoes and accessories for designer labels such as Pierre Cardin.

Footwear made in Menorca is still exported around the world along with high-quality leather clothing and accessories such as handbags, wallets and briefcases. You can shop in one of the fine boutiques in Maó or Ciutadella, or visit the factory shops (*see p147*) for bargains.

Ca Sa Pollaca

Handmade leather shoes, sandals and jackets since 1899 – and still at reasonable prices.
Carrer JM Quadrado 10, Ses Voltes, Ciutadella. Tel: 971 38 22 23.

Jaime Mascaró

Classy and fashionable leather shoes and clothes.
Carrer Ses Moreres 29, Maó. Tel: 971 36 05 68. www.jaimemascaro.com. Also at the airport, with a factory shop on the outskirts of Ferreries (see p147).

Looky Boutique

Expensive handbags and leather accessories. The factory shop is in Ciutadella.
Carrer de Ses Moreres 43, Maó. Tel: 971 36 06 48.

Pons Quintana

Quality leather shoes and accessories straight from the factory shop.
Carrer San Antonio 120, Alaior.
Tel: 971 37 10 50.
www.ponsquintana.com

Abarcas

The other side of the shoe industry is the opposite of this international market. The *abarca* (also spelt *avarca* and *avarque*) is unique to the Balearics and was originally designed for rustic workers, being both comfortable and hard-wearing, but today these sandals are worn by everyone.

The simple uppers, with a swatch of natural tanned nubuck leather across the bridge of the foot and a thong of the same leather behind the heel, is sewn to the sole with sturdy twine. The sole combines soft suede under the foot with a layer of car-tyre rubber underneath. This was meant to give the wearer grip on uneven terrain.

There are several producers of *abarcas* on the island and a few have got together to protect the quality of the product, joining forces with the Associació d'Empreses d'Artesania de Menorca. Two artisans who still produce by hand are:

Ca'n Doblas Artesania

Pretty and elegant sandals in a range of pastel colours and styles.
Plaça Jaume II 1, Ferreries. Tel: 971 15 50 21. www.candoblas.com

Uris Mercadal SL

Sophisticated take on *abarcas*; the style remains the same but the materials, patterns and pinks, purples and blues are unique.
Plaça Jaume II 10, Ciutadella.
Tel: 971 38 22 78.

Shoe shopping in Ciutadella

Entertainment

The quiet little sister of the Balearics, Menorca certainly doesn't have the same reputation as a party island as its larger siblings Ibiza and Mallorca. If you're after serious clubbing, you're in the wrong place. However, there are one or two late-night venues, and many large hotels also run discotheques during peak season. The main resort areas have karaoke bars or large-screen TVs that air popular soaps and live sports events.

BARS, CLUBS AND DISCOS

Clubs generally stay open until dawn and don't get busy until around midnight. Do what the locals do: have a late dinner around 10pm and then head to a bar to watch the nightly *paseo* (communal evening stroll). Spaniards go to clubs to be seen, not to drink till they drop – so dressing smartly is *de rigueur* to get into the best local places.

Maó

With the largest population on the island, Maó has Menorca's biggest concentration of clubs and bars. Although there are a couple of clubs up in town, most can be found along the waterside – pick the style of music you like and follow the beat!

Club Akelarre Jazz

Probably the coolest place on the island with ultra-modern, minimalist styling and jazz music.
Moll de Ponent 41–43. Tel: 971 36 50 70. Open: 8pm–late.

Mambo

Kick back at this late-night cocktail bar with a pretty terrace.
Moll de Llevant 209. Tel: 971 35 67 82.

Vineria Parra

Reggae, funk and hip-hop nights plus art exhibitions. The kitchen is open until 12.30am.
Carrer San Fernando 3.
Tel: 971 36 36 36.

Ciutadella

Asere

The premier salsa club in the city, with rooms cut into the cliffs by the harbour.
Carrer Pere Capllonc 15. Tel: 609 67 26 10. Open: daily in summer; weekends only in winter.

Lateral

Rock and techno for late-night dancing with über-cool local townies.
Es Pla de Sant Joan. Tel: 971 48 40 50. Open: May–Nov.

Pedros

Disco playing the hits of the '70s, '80s and '90s in affluent little Cala

Entertainment

Santandria, just down the road from Ciutadella. There is karaoke on Friday and Saturday.
Camí ses Vinyes, Cala Santandria. Open: Jun–Oct.

Cala'n Porter
Cova d'en Xoroi
The most famous club on the island, set in the vast cave complex above the resort of Cala'n Porter (*see p102*). Guest DJs appear throughout the summer and there is a bar with a perfect view of the sea during the day.
Cala'n Porter. Tel: 971 37 72 36. www.covadenxoroi.com. Open: bar 10am–9pm; disco 9pm–dawn. Admission charge includes a drink until 9pm.

Sant Climent
Casino de Sant Climent
Excellent jazz club with live sessions on Tuesdays from May to October; if you play an instrument, you can join in the evening jam sessions.
Carrer Sant Jaume 2–4. Tel: 971 15 34 18. www.casinosantcliment.com. Closed: Wed.

Sant Tomàs
Victory Club
This smart disco, decked out nautically with portholes and prints of Nelson, attracts all ages (mostly British and German tourists) and plays all the latest sounds. Open on Thursdays only during the summer.

Tapas bar on the promenade at Cala'n Bosch

Lord Nelson Apparthotel, Platja Sant Tomàs. Tel: 971 37 01 25.

CASINO
Maó
Casino Marítim

The only casino on the island also has a bar and restaurant. It is a great place for a little fling at the gaming tables and slot machines, but don't lose your shirt!

You will need some identification to gain admission, so don't forget to take your passport or driving licence with you.

Moll de Llevant 287. Tel: 971 36 49 62. www.grupocomar.com. Open: 9pm–5am.

HORSE SHOWS

The horse has an important place in traditional Catalan and Spanish life, and is a poignant emblem at many *festas* and religious celebrations. Try to catch the Festa de Sant Joan procession that takes place on 23 and 24 June in Ciutadella (*see p129*).

If you are not on the island at this time, there are two riding schools running dressage shows throughout the year. Both offer a rousing spectacle and are interesting for all ages.

Club Escola Menorquina is a family-owned company that has been running shows for over 25 years. These feature traditional precision horsemanship, including demonstrations of how the horses are trained for the *festas*, and impressive dressage tricks. *Carretera Cala Galdana, Ferreries; tel: 971 15 50*

59; www.showmenorca.com. Shows: Wed & Sun 8.30pm. Admission charge, free for under 12s.

Son Martorellet has a slightly different approach with a show of formal dressage and horse skills used on the mainland. The complex also has a small children's playground. *Carretera Cala Galdana, Km 1.7; tel: 609 04 94 93; www.sonmartorellet.com. Shows: Tue & Thur 8.30pm. Admission charge.*

MUSIC

Menorca has several well-established music festivals.

The main event is the Maó International Music Festival with performances from August to September. The Young Musicians of Maó are regular participants; international orchestras and choirs such as the English Chamber Orchestra and the American Spiritual Ensemble Choir have also performed. Most performances are in the Església de Santa Maria.

The Festival de Musica d'Estiu is held in July and August in Ciutadella each year, with the classical chamber and vocal performances usually held in the Claustre del Seminari at 9.30pm. More details can be had from the Tourist Office at Plaça de la Catedral (*tel: 971 38 26 93*). A classical music festival in Fornells also runs through July and August, with concerts held on five Thursdays across that time.

The Menorcan Jazz Festival is held in May with various performances at venues across the island. These include the cloister of Església San Francesc and Parc d'es Freginal in Maó, Plaça d'Espanya in Ferreries and Plaça de la Catedral in Ciutadella. The festival is sponsored by *Jazz Obert Magazine* (*Jazz Obert; tel: 666 37 39 61; www.jazzobert.com*).

Ongoing performances

The Augustine convent church of El Socors (*see p131*) in Ciutadella hosts concerts at 11.30am on Tuesdays to Thursdays, in June and September (*Carrer del Seminari 7; tel: 971 48 12 97; open: Tue–Sat 10.30am–1.30pm; admission charge*).

Església de Santa Maria in Maó (*see p40*) also holds organ recitals at 11.30am daily apart from Sunday between April and October (*Plaça de Constitució*).

Pedreres de S'Hostal quarry (*see pp125–6*) at Ciutadella (*Cami Vell; tel: 971 48 15 78*) has a small stone stage that hosts orchestral and musical concerts throughout the summer.

THEATRE AND THE ARTS

The island had two main theatres but at the time of writing they were both closed and facing uncertain futures (*see p20*).

There are spectacular horse shows on the island throughout the year

Children

Menorca is a great place to bring children on holiday. The island has guaranteed sunshine from May to September, warm seas for swimming, excellent sandy beaches for building sandcastles, and a range of watersports from pedalos to banana rides. Most of Menorca's beaches, except perhaps Son Bou (see pp112–13) and Sant Tomàs (see pp111–12), are good for youngsters because the shallows are gradual with no big waves – perfect for building confidence.

Menorca's well-established tourism infrastructure caters well to families. Most large hotel and apartment complexes have their own swimming pools, with a paddling pool for toddlers. Kids' clubs and in-complex entertainment ensure that they will rarely be bored and will have plenty of opportunities to make new friends. The island's larger western resorts, such as Cala'n Bosch and Cala'n Forcat, offer the added entertainment of water parks (*see pp119 & 120*).

Getting out on the water on boat trips is great fun for children of all ages, and there are glass-bottom boat trips from Maó harbour that allow them to get a fish's-eye view of life beneath the waves. Older children might like to have a go at snorkelling – the instruction is professional and instructors are English or English-speaking.

Children can spend their well-earned pocket money on the latest holiday fashions – like having a temporary henna tattoo or, for the girls, getting hair braids put in.

The *festas* that take place across the island throughout the summer will certainly catch their attention with local traditional costumes and dancing (*see pp26–7*). If you can't be there on 23 and 24 June for the famous Sant Joan celebrations in Ciutadella (*see p129*), visit one of the two entertaining horse shows where the animals are put through their paces in preparation for the big day (*see p154*). Children will be enthralled by the equine tricks – although they may all leave the stadium wanting riding lessons!

A WORD ABOUT THE SUN

Don't forget to keep young skin well protected, as the sun is very strong here, especially between June and September. Always put sunblock on children after they have been swimming. Make sure they wear a hat and carry a long-sleeved top in case you need to cover sunburnt limbs. Children also need to be kept well hydrated in the hot weather. They may not complain about feeling thirsty but regular drinks are the order of the day.

The Spanish love children and treat them with indulgence. They are welcomed in restaurants and bars, and are even spirited away by waiters into the kitchens for mama to pat them on the head, and coo over them. Boisterous behaviour is not frowned upon as it is in some other countries, and youngsters are allowed to run around while the adults chat to one another over drinks.

Spanish children regularly stay up until after midnight, especially during the long summer holidays, but don't forget that they will have had at least two hours' sleep during the traditional afternoon siesta in the heat of the early afternoon. It may be wise to get your little ones into the same habit if you want to have an evening out in Spanish style.

Children

Menorca's beaches are perfect for sandcastle building

Sport and leisure

There is plenty to do on the island, although many of the activities are water-based. The great thing is that some of the most satisfying activities don't cost the earth and you can get to see the best that Menorca has to offer under your own steam. Organised activities are professionally managed, and most guides and instructors speak good English.

SPECTATOR SPORTS
Football
The football-crazy Catalans have no team in Menorca, though Mallorca has one. Instead, the island follows the action on TV. Some of the spectator sports on offer are described below.

Golf
The 18-hole course at Son Parc is not on the grand international tour but hosts the Menorca Men's Open Championship during the middle of May for a week. Later in the year it runs more competitions during October Golf Week (usually at the beginning of the month). There are local competitions every weekend and if you have a handicap you are welcome to enter. *Urbanización Son Parc. Tel: 971 35 90 59. www.golfsonparc.com. Open: daily.*

Regattas
There are several regattas throughout the year in the waters around the island.

Watching the action can be difficult from dry land, but when the boats dock at the end of the racing day the atmosphere along the harbourfront is magical.

The most important is the Menorca Sant Joan Regatta to coincide with the Sant Joan celebrations on 23 and 24 June (*see p129*). Boats race from Barcelona to Es Port in Maó (*www. regatamenorcasantjoan.com*). The King's Cup for traditional boats (Copa del Rey de Barcos de Época), held in late August at Maó harbour, is a colourful sight, heaving with classic wooden vessels (*www.velaclasicamenorca.com*).

Running
The Menorca half-marathon is usually held in Ciutadella in the first week of October. Runners start and finish at Plaça d'es Born (*see pp126–8*). *www.mitjamenorca.com*

Trotting races
Hippodromes in Maó and Ciutadella are the homes of weekly trotting races

(where horses pull two-wheeled lightweight carriages).

Hipódromo Municipal de Maó
Avinguda JA Clavé 400. Tel: 971 36 86 62. Open: May–Oct Sat from 5.30pm; Nov–Apr Sun from 11.30am.
Hipòdrom de Ciutadella
Carrer de s'Hipódromo. Tel: 971 38 80 38. www.hipodromdeciutadella.com. Open: Sun evenings 6pm.

SPORTS AND ACTIVITIES
Boat trips
Heading out onto the warm waters of the Mediterranean is one of the pleasures of a trip to Menorca, and many of the island's remote coves can only be reached by boat. There are numerous organised day trips from tourist harbours with swimming included. Simply take along your swimsuits and enjoy.

Blue Mediterraneum
Enjoy a day's sailing on a 23m (75ft) catamaran (*trips depart from the harbour at Maó; Tue–Sun 10.15am; lunch included*). For a more private experience, the company offers a full or half-day charter or champagne lunch with a range of boats to suit all budgets, tastes and group sizes.

There are also Blue Mediterraneum boats available for excursions at Ciutadella harbour, the port at Fornells, in the marina at Cala'n Bosch, and along the beach at Cala Galdana.
Tel: 609 30 53 14.
www.chartermenorca.com
Catamaran Charter
A choice of trips along the north shore of Menorca from the pretty fishing village of Fornells. In case of rough weather at sea, the cats will sail around the Badia de Fornells. You can also hire

The 18-hole golf course at Son Parc

kayaks and there are romantic daily sunset sails as well.
Maritimo des Fornells.
Passeig Marítim. Tel: 628 48 64 26.
www.catamarancharter.net

Cycling

Quiet and relatively flat roads away from the main roads offer some lovely cycling routes. From Ciutadella north to the cluster of resorts around Cala'n Forcat (*see p120*) or to the lighthouse at Punta Nati (*see p129*), or south to Cala'n Bosch (*see p119*), even beginners won't get out of breath. There are similar trails around Fornells, Arenal d'en Castell, Es Grau and along the back roads of the south coast; they are all very clearly signposted. The cycling is more challenging inland or among the *barrancas* of the south-coast resorts (*see p100*), where the way down is easy but you have no option but to pedal up on the way out.

If you are an experienced mountain biker, the narrow country lanes and walking trails offer the most adventure, but it is the beautiful surroundings rather than the degree of difficulty that is the draw.

Dia Complert Adventure Sports
(*on the waterfront, Passeig Marítim 41, Fornells; tel: 609 67 09 96; www.diacomplert.com*) offers guided mountain-bike treks, or you can hire a bike and set off on your own adventure. They also sell second-hand bikes and hire out kayaks for blading around the bay.

In late October the Menorcan Touring Cycling Association (*www. ciclomenorca.com*) organises the Vuelta Cicloturistica – a three-stage race around the island open to everyone.

Diving

Menorca has worked hard to maintain the purity of its marine environment and certainly has something to offer every diver, from caves to shipwrecks. The quality of diving training is good, and qualified divers can choose from

Learn to dive in Cala Galdana

several locations for guided or accompanied dives.

Most diving companies run an 'introduction to diving' package that is a kind of appetiser session. To gain the Open Water Certificate, the first-stage qualification, usually takes around five days of study and practical training.

Addaia

ULMO Diving Addaia Good diving outfit on the northeast coast.
Zona Comercial Addaia. Tel: 971 35 90 05. www.ulmodiving.com

Cala Galdana

SUBmorena Divers Diving instruction and trips on the south coast.
Passeig del Riu 7. Tel: 609 30 37 60.

Cala'n Porter

Dive Cala Blanca An English-speaking and accredited PADI training centre.
Dive Cala Blanca, Cala Blanca. Tel: 617 65 69 06. www.divecalablanca.com

Fornells

Diving Centre Fornells Training and diving equipment on rental.
Passeig Marítim 68. Tel: 971 37 64 31. www.divingfornells.com

S'Algar

S'Algar Diving Menorca A professional company offering water-based activities, including diving training, parascending and powerboat lessons.
Passeig Marítim. Tel: 971 15 06 01. www.salgardiving.com

Glass-bottom boat trips

If swimming under the waves isn't for you, it is possible to enjoy the varied sea life around the Menorcan coast on a glass-bottom boat trip. The viewing windows allow you to see shoals of fish darting among the rocks, and also crustaceans and corals on the sea bottom.

Amigos

Runs trips with stops for swimming: the boat has a waterslide and a bar/café.
Cala'n Bosch. Tel: 618 34 80 06. Trips: daily in season 9am & 2pm. Tickets must be purchased at least an hour before departure.

Don Joan

Take a tour of the outer harbour at Maó with an English commentary. You'll see Illa del Llatzeret, Golden Farm and La Mola, all historic buildings related to the British naval base here (*see pp62–3*). On other days the boat hosts swimming trips up the coast around Es Grau or Binibeca.
Departure: Port de Maó. Tel: 971 35 07 78. Harbour tours: Tue & Sat 11.30am, 1pm & 2.30pm. Coastal tours: Apr–Oct Mon, Wed–Fri & Sun 9.45am & 2.45pm.

Yellow Catamarans

The same harbour tour as Don Joan (*see above*) but in a cute yellow craft.
Port de Maó. Tel: 639 67 63 51. www.yellowcatamarans.com. Departures: Mon–Sat every 45 mins from 10.30am–3.30pm. Also May–Oct Sun 10.45am, 12.15pm & 1.45pm.

Sport and leisure

Golf

Surprisingly, there is only one golf course on the island and it is located at Son Parc on the north coast (*see p95*). The golf school has English-speaking teachers and 'Swingcam' stance analysis to improve your game. Children's lessons are also provided. Book in advance if you want to play a round on the 18-hole course – club rules dictate that you should not turn up in beach clothes.

Urbanización Son Parc.
Tel: 971 35 90 59. www.golfsonparc.com.
Open: daily.

Horse riding

The Camí de Cavalls is an ancient bridle path running around the coastline (*see box, p144*), perfect for gentle hacks through the beautiful Menorcan countryside. Pony and horse hire, as well as riding lessons, are available from the following centres:

Parts of Menorca are ideally suited to windsurfing

Can Pouny

Classes and pony trekking for all ages are offered at this friendly place. English and Spanish are spoken.
Carretera Maó–Fornells, Km 5.
Tel: 971 37 16 51 Open: daily in season.

Stables Farm

Novice and experienced, family and group rides. Try the ride down to the remote Cales Coves (*see p104*) to see hidden Menorca.
Carretera ME12, Cala'n Porter Sant Climent, Km 7.6. Tel: 971 15 32 00.
Open: daily in season.

Picadero Menorca

Lessons and pony trekking.
Carretera Alaior–Son Bou (just off the roundabout beneath the ME1). Tel: 608 32 35 66. Open: daily in season.

Sea kayaking

With benign summer waters and miles of breathtaking coastline to explore, it is not surprising that sea kayaking has become popular very quickly here. If you need some training, the bay at Fornells is the perfect location; once you have got your sea legs you are free to explore caverns and remote bays that you can't reach by road.

Boating is a great way to view the coastline

Dia Complert Adventure Sports (*see p160*) offers accompanied sea-kayaking safaris around the Menorca coastline or has kayaks for hire if you are already proficient.

Snorkelling
The clear waters around Menorca's coves are ideal for snorkelling. No need for supervision or tuition; just make sure that kids know how to breathe through the tube. You can swim out along the banks of the *calas* to spot shrimp, crabs, the occasional squid or octopus and, of course, lots of fish. It is a wonderfully relaxing way to spend a couple of hours.

Walking and hiking
Menorca has a network of well-marked walking routes and relatively flat countryside, so it is an excellent environment for hiking. There are well-signposted coastal routes (try the Camí de Cavalls, *see p144*) and inland routes with ancient remains and rural lifestyles to explore. There are also lots of hidden beaches that can only be reached on foot or by boat. If you prefer walking with a guide, Dia Complert Adventure Sports (*see p160*) offers trekking and hiking.

Windsurfing
Fornells
One of the best places in the Mediterranean to learn to windsurf is in the Badia de Fornells (*see pp86–7*). The wide shallow waters and prevailing breezes offer ideal conditions and the instruction is excellent. If you already know how to windsurf, there are plenty of rental boards here too.

Windsurf Fornells Tuition and hire at the entrance to the village.
Passeig Marítim. Tel: 971 18 81 50.
www.windfornells.com

Son Xoriguer, Cala'n Bosch
Surf & Sail Menorca Sailing and windsurfing school.
Apartment 257, Urbanización Son Xoriguer. Tel: 971 38 71 05.
www.surfsailmenorca.com

Ciutadella harbour
Sports Massanet Tuition and boat hire for experienced sailors.
Carrer Marina 66. Tel: 971 48 21 86.

Yachting

Swap your land-based holiday in a hotel, apartment or villa for a water-based stay. The magnificent coastline and easy passage to the sister Balearic Islands of Ibiza, Mallorca and Formentera, combined with benign summer waters, make Menorca a prime sailing destination of the world.

You don't even need to head out of Menorcan waters to reap the benefit of a sailing holiday. Some of the island's most unspoilt *calas* are best reached by boat (such as Cales Coves, *see p104*), and there can be no better feeling than dropping anchor in your own private cove surrounded by crystal-clear azure waters with a hint of golden sand, where the only sound you hear is the lapping of the waves.

MARINAS

Marinas in Menorca vary in size and in facilities. The most basic offer berths and fresh water, while the most modern have electrical connections for boats, shower facilities and shops. The most romantic ports of call are those like Fornells, where you can disembark and sit on the quayside enjoying an aperitif or dinner at a restaurant overlooking the boats.

Popular marinas
Addaia (*see pp85–6*)
Cala'n Bosch (*see pp119–20*)
Cala Galdana (*see pp102–4*)
Ciutadella (*see pp123–4*)
Fornells (*see pp90–91*)
Maó (*see pp40–42*)

GETTING ORGANISED

A popular choice for beginners or those after fun is the flotilla holiday. Groups of boats sail together on a set route, usually with a guide. If you have a Day Skipper Certificate (*see below*), you can crew a boat yourself (this is called a bare boat). With no certificate, you need to hire a captain.

Sunsail have a good deal of experience in holiday provision for both flotilla and bare-boat yachting. *Contact them at: The Port House, Port Solent, Portsmouth, Hampshire PO6 4TH. Tel: 0870 777 0313. Fax: 023 9221 9827. www.sunsail.com*

Menorca has a multitude of companies offering boat rentals, package tours or crewed boats for those with or without a Day Skipper Certificate. **Blue Mediterraneum** offers crewed and bare boats from around 9–23m (30–75ft). *Port de Maó. Tel: 609 30 53 14. www.chartermenorca.com*

TRAINING
The Day Skipper Certificate

This certificate gives the skipper responsibility for the safety of the boat and crew for daytime sailing in local waters (not out in the open ocean) and requires basic yachting skills in moderate wind and sea conditions. Normally, study for the certificate takes five days or three weekends on board a boat, and teaches basic navigation skills, chart work, boat handling and maintenance.

Menorca Cruising School and Yacht Charter

This company offers sailing lessons from a day's introduction to sailing for

complete novices, a two-day novice's course or a five-day Royal Yachting Association approved course. Instructors all speak excellent English. They have boats for hire for those with their Day Skipper or Yachtmaster's certificates.
Tel: 971 38 90 03.
www.menorcasailing.co.uk

Join the yachties in Maó harbour

Birdwatching

While the whole island of Menorca was made a Biosphere Reserve in 1993 to counter the adverse effect of tourism, Parc Naturel de S'Albufera des Grau (*see pp92–5*) was the first area to receive extra protection as it is one of the most important wetland areas in the Balearics. Today the saltwater wetlands at Son Bou (*see pp112–13*) on the south coast have also been accorded conservation status, and the marshy strip behind the beach is once more teeming with animal and birdlife as well as flora. The rest of the island is also an important birding site for both native species and visiting breeders from the north and south, plus migrants crossing the Mediterranean in the spring and autumn.

Parc Naturel de S'Albufera des Grau is a multi-environment region, including woodland, meadows and a 70-hectare (17-acre) freshwater lagoon, which acts as a magnet for

S'Albufera des Grau Natural Park is the subject of a massive conservation programme

fowl like coots, mallards and pochards, and wading birds such as herons and egrets. These include the numerous cattle egret and blue heron, but also the rarer night and squacco herons. Stilts are also common in the muddy shallows.

The woodlands are home to many species, including the tiny firecrest, the smallest European bird. Warblers and crakes can usually be heard rather than seen, and this is especially true of the polyphonic nightingale. Various species of owl hunt by night, while during the day you may see the elegant flight of the booted eagle as it swoops low across the water. During spring and autumn, the park is teeming with life. It acts as a welcome stopover for many species on longer journeys north or south.

Another enclosed cove, this time with high cliffs, is the inlet at Cala Galdana (*see pp102–4*). Birds such as Cetti's warblers and nightingales are abundant here, and it is also a nesting site for thousands of swifts who stay for the summer.

The protected saltwater wetlands at Son Bou are Menorca's largest reed beds, although there are several smaller beds dotting the island. Warblers are the most common

A young night heron

species here, including the common great reed warbler. The multicoloured bee-eater is one of Menorca's spectacular migratory birds, arriving every year from the Sahara.

Cap de Cavalleria (*see pp138–40*) is less settled by man than other parts of the island, and there are several good vantage points to watch curlews and ospreys, plus the Audouin's Gull, one of the world's rarest gull species.

Head to the Punta de S'Escullar in the far northwest to find the nesting areas of the Balearic shearwater and the heavier Cory's, both large seabird species that spend much of their lives out at sea. The cliffs are also home to Alpine swifts and a few *miloca* (Egyptian vultures).

Menorca has a particularly varied population of predator birds for such a small island. Although pressure on their habitat has reduced the numbers, you can be sure to see at least one large raptor. As well as the Egyptian vulture, the booted eagle, osprey and red kite also catch the thermals, while smaller falcons, kestrels and marsh harriers hunt in the lower skies and across the fields.

USEFUL ORGANISATIONS
Dia Complert Adventure Sports
Offers specialist birdwatching tours (*see p160*).
Passeig Marítim 41, Fornells. Tel: 609 67 09 96. www.diacomplert.com

The website *www.birdingpal.org* puts avid birders around the world in touch with one another to share information and meet up for organised activities.

The Royal Society for the Protection of Birds (RSPB)
Information and activities for birdwatchers with affiliations to international organisations.
The Lodge, Sandy, Beds, SG19 2DL. Tel: 01767 680551. www.rspb.org.uk

Food and drink

A small island surrounded by water, the seafood in Menorca is always fresh and varied, and includes grilled sardines and swordfish, flambéed shrimps, squid and shellfish. Caldereta de llagosta *(a rich lobster stew, see p90) is the pièce de résistance of Menorcan cuisine, and Fornells has a particular reputation for the dish, which is priced at around €60 per person. The* caldetera de mariscos *(stew of mixed fish) is cheaper and just as delicious.*

WHAT TO EAT

The island offers a good variety for meat eaters too. Succulent beef and lamb are supplemented by game such as rabbit, partridge and quail. Barbecuing is the most popular method of cooking, but there are also a good number of slow-cooked stews that see the population through the winter.

Island specialities include *sopas mallorquinas* (a thick soup with garlic, olives, vegetables and occasionally pork) and the ubiquitous Queso de Mahón, Menorcan cheese (*see pp116–17*), plus a range of air-dried hams and salamis. Paella is also on many menus. This traditional Catalan dish of rice, beans and peppers, flavoured with saffron and featuring both meat and seafood, is the most famous dish of southern mainland Spain. Tapas – small 'bites' of various tasty dishes such as *calamari* (squid in batter) and *patatas bravas* (potatoes fried in paprika and garlic) – are available all over the island and make a good lunchtime or early evening snack.

Larger portions of tapas are called *raciones* and can be ordered in multiples to make up a substantial meal.

Vegetarian food

Pescetarians won't have a problem, as the fresh seafood is delicious and served all around the island. Many tapas are non-meat items and you can easily find non-meat pastas and pizzas, but be aware that even if a restaurant is willing

Home-cured hams hanging in Grill Las Brassas, Los Delfines

to serve you paella without the chicken, the dish will probably have been cooked in chicken stock. The same may be true of some soups, though the locals have a range of non-meat versions.

True vegetarians and vegans may have more of a problem. *Tumbet* – a stew of vegetables in tomato sauce or *samfiana (see box)* – is a possibility, but that's about it. Good salads are getting easier to come by but are normally served as an accompaniment to a main dish; however, most restaurants will happily do their best to accommodate your requests.

DRINKS

Spanish coffee (*café*) is short, strong and black. Ask for a *café grande con leche* if you want a longer, milkier version.

Beer (*cerveza*) is a lager type – look for Spanish San Miguel.

For something a little stronger, Xoriguer produce a range of gins and liqueurs (*see pp172–3*). Most Spanish wine is imported from the mainland and is of reasonable quality, although there are now a couple of bodegas in Menorca. Bubbly cava makes a great aperitif, as does sherry served ice cold, while brandy rounds off a long supper perfectly. It tends to be a little softer and fruitier than its French counterpart.

WHEN TO EAT

The Spanish traditionally eat lunch around 1pm, then head home for a siesta. They don't eat dinner until around 10pm and most restaurants

COMMON FOOD TERMS

Carne	meat
Peix	fish
Huevos	eggs
Queso	cheese
Arros	rice
Fruta	fruit
Verduras	vegetables
Jamon	ham
Chorizo	spicy sausage
Bocadillos	sandwiches
Estramesos	plate of meats and cheeses
Carn d'oila	soup of different meats
Escudella	vegetable soup
Samfiana	slow-cooked onions, peppers, aubergines and tomatoes
Sopas mallorquinas	vegetable soup (sometimes has meat)
Arros negra	rice cooked with black squid ink
Arros a banda	rice with seafood
Paella	aromatic rice and vegetables cooked with seafood such as prawns and mussels (sometimes chicken)
Sobrasada	spicy pork sausage
Greixonera de peix	fish stew
Panades sobrasada	savoury pastry with meat or fish
Xurros	sweet fried doughnuts served on sticks

outside the tourist resort areas won't open until 8pm. If you want authentic Menorcan atmosphere, stave off your hunger pangs with a few portions of *tapas* in the early evening.

WHERE TO EAT

There's no shortage of British and Euro-cuisine in the major resorts. The curry, schnitzel and pizza menus many restaurants provide is pretty much standard. Look beyond these venues for some superlative food across the island.

The following price guide is for dinner for one person without drinks:

£	under €15
££	€15–25
£££	€25–35
££££	over €35

Alaior
The Cobblers Garden Restaurant ££££

Arguably one of the best restaurants on the island, hidden away in a smart town house that was once the home of a famous local shoemaker – hence the name – and now owned by Brits. Weather permitting, traditional Menorcan menus are served in the delightful courtyard. There are some vegetarian options and a good wine list.
Carrer San Macario 6. Tel: 971 37 14 00. www.thecobblers.es. Open: Apr–Sept Mon–Sat 7pm–late. Closed: Oct–Mar. Advance booking recommended.

Cala'n Bosch
Aquarium £££

A sublime seafood restaurant sitting at the end of the right-hand side of the marina, and taking its name from the massive fish tanks at the back of the dining room. Choose from bowls of steaming muscles or lobster stew, and accompany with a fine dry white wine. Service is precise and friendly and the atmosphere buzzes.
Es Lago. Tel: 971 38 74 42. Open: daily 10.30am–11pm.

Ciutadella
Café Balear £££

By far the most popular restaurant on the harbourfront. There are a few tables by the quayside plus more inside and a throng of hungry and well-heeled locals waiting to grab them. The seafood comes in daily on the owner's boat, the *Rosa Santa*. Book or get there early.
Es Pla de Sant Joan 15, Port de Ciutadella. Tel: 971 38 00 05. Open: daily 7–11.30pm.

Cas Cònsol £££

Sophisticated bar and restaurant serving modern Mediterranean food, with perfect views overlooking the harbour. There's a tiny terrace twinkling with fairy lights; absolutely the right place for a romantic supper.
Plaça d'es Born 17. Tel: 971 48 46 54. Open: daily noon–4pm & 7pm–1am.

Es Grau
Bar Restaurant Tamarindos ££

Enjoy a quiet lunch of tapas on the terrace or watch the sun disappear over a platter of fresh prawns. The best place to relax and round off a day's healthy walking in the Parc Naturel de S'Albufera des Grau (*see pp92–5*).
Pas des Tamarrells 14. Tel: 971 35 94 20. Open: daily noon–4pm & 5–10.30pm.

Ferreries
Liorna £££

This elegant gem of a town-house restaurant with a lovely garden is hidden down a backstreet in the old part of town. The emphasis is on sourcing local produce, with wonderful

seafood and pizzas on offer, and cocktails made from local Xorigeur gin (*see pp172–3*) at the pretty bar.
Carrer Econom Florit 9. Tel: 971 37 39 12. Open: daily 7–11pm.

Fornells
Es Cranc ££
This beautifully-styled traditional dining room just a couple of minutes along the route to the Fornells tower (*see p91*) offers excellent seafood, including live crab and delicious *caldereta de llagosta*. There is no terrace, outdoor chairs or sea views, just tremendous home cooking.
Calle Escoles 31. Tel: 971 37 64 42. Open: mid-Mar–mid-Oct daily 1.30–4pm & 8pm–midnight.

El Pescador £££
Fornells' most popular restaurant has wicker chairs overlooking the water, a manic atmosphere, and a wide variety of fish and seafood dishes as well as the ubiquitous *caldereta*. Diners are given paper bibs to prevent splashback and the place is always heaving! Booking advised for the evening and also for weekend lunchtimes.
Carrer de S'Algaret 3. Tel: 971 37 65 38. Open: daily noon–midnight.

Maó
S'Espigó ££
Established for close to 35 years, this place is famed for its excellent fish and seafood dishes, and is justifiably popular with a loyal local clientele. The atmosphere is elegant and sophisticated. Bookings are advisable at weekends.
Moll de Llevant 267. Tel: 971 36 99 09. Open: Feb–Dec Tue–Sun 1–5pm & 8pm–midnight.

La Tropical ££
A tiny dining room and just a few outdoor tables off busy Carrer Ses Moreres, this charismatic Spanish restaurant serves some of the freshest fish in town. Try the 'menu from the market', which changes daily.
Carrer La Lluna 36. Tel: 971 36 05 56. Open: daily 1–4pm & 7.30pm–midnight.

Sant Climent
Musupta Cusi £
Traditional restaurant run in irrepressible style in a traditional Menorcan farmhouse with jamming sessions on piano and drums most days. Go for a lunch of quality tapas on the romantic terrace by night.
Tel: 646 67 86 44 (mobile). Open: daily noon–4pm & 7.30pm–midnight. Booking advised.

Sant Lluís
Restaurante Pan y Vino ££££
An ex-professional musician turned wine aficionado and his partner offer an intimate dining experience in a converted Menorcan farmhouse or outside on the garden terrace. See if you can spot any famous faces.
Camí de la Coixa 3, Torret. Tel: 971 15 03 22. www.panyvinomenorca.com. Open: Jun–Sept Sat–Wed 8–11pm. Booking essential.

Menorcan gin

When the British arrived on Menorca they made many far-reaching changes. One was the development of gin distillation, which created a product that is still inexorably linked to the island.

Maó became one of the Royal Navy's primary Mediterranean bases and the port was teeming with naval personnel. The English sailors who frequented the taverns of the port during the 18th century were hard drinkers. Back in England the latest fashion was for gin – alcohol produced by distilling malt or grain and infusing juniper berries – but there wasn't a supply in the Balearics and it seems that nothing else would do. Spotting an opportunity to make a killing, Menorcan entrepreneurs began importing the raw materials for gin distillation and set to work satisfying the demand.

There was one huge difference between the gins produced in northern Europe and Mahón gin (as it became known). This local gin used grape distillates mixed with juniper berries, which imparts a different kind of flavour from the very crisp English style. It is more akin to a Dutch *genever*.

The British introduced gin to Menorca

The Xoriguer brand

The Pons family had been millers on the island and owned a mill called Xoriguer. When they decided to go into the distilling business, they named the business after the mill and Distilerias Xoriguer was born.

Miquel Pons Justo (1906–81) was a master marketing man before the term was even invented and moved the brand to its dominant position today. He made the decision to continue with the traditional distillation methods and old-style pottery jugs called *canecas* (traditionally these were adopted because they were strong enough to make the sea crossing when the gin was exported).

Xoriguer is still a family-owned business (*see pp38–9*), and only the heirs to the legacy know the precise recipe for Xoriguer gin.

Quality control

Mahón Gin, made by Xoriguer, is one of only two gins produced in Europe, the other being Plymouth in the UK, to have a specific appellation – or EU designation of origin – meaning it can only be made on the island according to a specific distillation process. This guarantees the quality of the product and protects the product from fraudsters and imitators.

Enjoy!

Xoriguer's complex aromatic flavour and fruity wine base mean that it provides an excellent base for cocktails. Traditionally it is drunk at Menorcan fiestas with home-made lemonade in a drink called *pomada*, or with just a splash of soda water and a slice of lemon in *pallofa*. It can also be drunk neat over ice.

Xoriguer produce a ready-made *pomada* so you don't have to mix it yourself. They also produce a range of liqueurs unique to the company, including *calent* and *pago*.

Calent is a traditional drink originally made by the farmer's wife in the kitchen. It had no set recipe, being an infusion of various wild herbs, aniseed and cinnamon with wine so each batch would taste slightly different. Xoriguer now produce *calent* to a secret but standard recipe.

Pago is a drink that was originally brought to the island by the Phoenicians. The liqueur has a base of gentian and herbs and is usually mixed with four parts gin to one part *pago* to make a pleasant, refreshing cocktail.

Distilerias Xoriguer: Moll de Ponent 91, Maó. Tel: 971 36 21 97. www.xoriguer.es. Open: Jun–Sept Mon–Fri 8am–7pm, Sat 9am–1pm; Oct–May Mon–Fri 9am–1pm & 4–7pm.

Accommodation

Menorca has a wide range of accommodation to suit all budgets and families, but finding rooms as an independent traveller can be difficult, especially in summer, as so many hotels are contracted to the major travel companies. High rates for walk-in clients make it more expensive than booking a package with flights and accommodation combined. You will need to book well in advance for the school holidays in July and August.

Most hotels have excellent facilities and many are aimed at families, offering kids' clubs and on-site entertainment, but there are sedate options if you are looking for a peaceful break. Maó and Ciutadella have smart urban hotels that are useful bases for sightseeing.

Escape the crowds by booking into an *agrotourism* – a farmhouse or villa offering B&B accommodation in rural areas. These properties have charm and character and allow greater independence than all-in deals at resort hotels. For even more independence, try self-catering accommodation in purpose-built complexes or villas with private pools and gardens. **H & GC Villas** (*Barn House Lodge, Barn House Lane, Pulborough, West Sussex RH20 2BS; tel: 07711 168148; www. menorcanvillas.info*) is a small company run by a couple who are very familiar with Menorca. They organise villa and farmhouse rentals at highly competitive prices.

For upper-end holiday lets, it's worth contacting *www.meonvillas.co.uk* or *www.jamesvillas.co.uk*

Menorca is so small that nowhere is very far away. This is a destination where you can have one base and still easily explore the rest of the island.

WHERE TO STAY

The following list is a mix of urban hotels, tourist complexes and agrotourist accommodation across the island. Price scales are for a high-season (Jul & Aug) double room and breakfast only unless stated.

£	up to €100 per night
££	€100–150 per night
£££	over €150 per night

Cala Galdana
Cala Galdana Hotel & Villas d'Aljandar £££
Modern hotel and self-catering apartments in manicured grounds with a shady pool fringed with palms just a minute from the sea. This is a

good option for families with young teenagers as there are lots of cafés and snack bars within the complex and there's plenty of safe fun to be had on and around the beach.

Cala Galdana, Ferreries.
Tel: 971 15 45 00.
www.hotelcalagaldana.com

Cala Morell

Hotel Rural Sant Ignasi £££

Hidden down winding Menorcan lanes in rolling parkland, the Sant Ignasi is in a beautiful 18th-century mansion painted warm yellow. The 20 rooms are large and individually furnished with period and modern pieces. The luxurious feel is carried through to the gastronomic restaurant, the romantic terrace and the good-sized pool. The perfect place to relax.

Carretera Cala Morell. Tel: 971 38 55 75.
www.santignasi.com

Cala'n Bosch

Viva Menorca Apartments £

Five smart blocks surrounding a lagoon-shaped swimming pool. Self-catering is an option but the hotel has a restaurant with a pretty terrace. There's Wi-Fi, a sauna and entertainment at the bar most nights; otherwise the bustling marina is a ten-minute walk away. The rooms at the front of the hotel get a lot of traffic noise, so ask to be by the pool.

Calle Llevant. Tel: 971 38 78 43.
www.hotelsviva.com

Balconies overlooking the sea at Cala Galdana Hotel

Cala'n Porter
Hotel Sa Barrera ££
This addition to Menorca's hotel scene is lavishly Moroccan in theme, with ornate gilt ceilings and wrought ironwork. The terrace has a superb view of the little beach and a small pool to splash around in, while the 26 rooms are spacious and beautifully furnished. Sample the Italian cuisine and sit back with a cocktail or two.
Calle Sa Barrera 12. Tel: 971 37 71 26.

Ciutadella
Hotel Madrid £
This villa-style hotel is located in a residential street west of the centre. Rooms are plain but clean and comfortable and the downstairs restaurant and bar is reliably good. The hotel's facilities include a small swimming pool.
Calle Madrid 60. Tel: 971 38 03 28. www.hotelmadridmenorca.com. Open: Apr–Oct.

Hotel Port Ciutadella £££
A sleek urban choice overlooking the sea at Platja Gran, ten minutes' walk away from the centre of chic Ciutadella. Rooms are spacious and ultra-modern, with spotless white bed linen and splashes of rich colour. The swimming pool is surrounded by decking, the spa is complete with sauna, steam bath, Jacuzzi and massage treatments, and there's a choice of bars and restaurants. There's an underground car park, and easy access to the beaches of the west and south coasts.

Passeig Marítim 36. Tel: 971 48 25 20. www.sethotels.com

Es Mercadal
Hotel Es Mercadal ££
A stylishly renovated traditional town house in the middle of sleepy Es Mercadal. There are six smartly fitted bedrooms all with state-of-the-art en-suites, a TV room, a little terrace bar and a tiled dining room. An excellent place to sample the Menorca of yesteryear without forsaking creature comforts, and an ideal base for touring the island.
Carrer Nou 49. Tel: 971 37 83 17. www.hotelesmercadel.com

Biniarroca Hotel Rural, Sant Lluís

The Hotel Santo Tomàs

Fornells
Hostal Fornells £

This is an excellent choice for euro economisers. Located in the centre of town, rooms are modern, albeit small, with pine furniture and pastel-coloured fabrics; most have private balconies with sea views. The en-suite bathrooms boast tubs as well as showers. Breakfast is enjoyed on a pleasant terrace with arches overlooking the pool.
Calle Mayor 17. Tel: 971 37 66 76.
www.hostalfornells.com

Maó
Hotel Port Mahón £££

Perched above Maó harbour and tucked in a quiet backstreet, this elegant colonial-style hotel offers smart rooms with terraces and balconies as well as a swimming pool, late-night piano bar and sun terrace overlooking the sea. Great for a weekend treat – the service is charming and efficient too.
Avinguda del Port de Maó.
Tel: 971 36 26 00. www.sethotels.com

Sant Lluís
Biniarroca Hotel Rural ££–£££

This 15th-century whitewashed farmhouse is overrun with purple bougainvillea and was one of Menorca's first boutique hotels. There are well-designed rooms with flower-strewn terraces in the garden extension and older rooms stuffed with antiques in the house. The property has two pools, a verdant garden, Wi-Fi and a great restaurant open in the evenings. It's just the place for honeymooners.
Camí Vell 57. Tel: 971 15 00 59.
www.biniarroca.com

Sant Tomàs
Hotel Santo Tomàs ££

Sitting in neat gardens overlooking the sea and a great stretch of sandy beach, this modern hotel has a beauty centre, a library and two pools. The restaurant Costa Sur has a great menu and a terrace for special occasions. Good for families with children as the hotel backs on to the beach.
Platja de Sant Tomàs, Es Migjorn Gran.
Tel: 971 37 00 25. www.sethotels.com

Practical guide

Arriving

Entry formalities

Citizens of EU Schengen Agreement countries need only a picture ID to gain entry to any part of Spain. Residents of the following countries need a valid passport: the UK, Switzerland, Australia, Canada, New Zealand and the USA. All other nationalities should consult their nearest Spanish Embassy.

Arriving by air

Menorca's International Airport (*tel: 971 15 70 00; www.aena.es*) is 15 minutes inland from Maó.

Scheduled services: **Iberia Airlines** (*www.iberia.es*) is the Spanish national air carrier and it has regular services from Menorca to locations on the other Balearic Islands, on mainland Spain and within Europe. Flights to European cities normally include a transfer in Barcelona.

Flying to Menorca from the UK is easy: **British Airways** flies scheduled flights to Maó from Gatwick (*www.britishairways.com*). Budget carriers from the UK include **easyJet**, which flies scheduled flights from Bristol, Liverpool, Heathrow, Gatwick, Manchester and Newcastle (*www.easyjet.com*). **Jet2** flies to Maó from Newcastle, Edinburgh, Leeds and Belfast (*www.jet2.com*). **Monarch** flies to Maó from Manchester, Luton and London Gatwick (*www.flymonarch.com*).

If you are travelling from North America or Australasia, the simplest option is to fly into Madrid or Barcelona on mainland Spain and then a transfer flight on to Maó. **Qantas** (*www.qantas.co.uk*) and **American Airlines** (*www.americanairlines.co.uk*) offer scheduled services to both destinations, while Iberia and SpanAir (*www.spanair.com*) provide the link into Maó. Consult a travel agent or website such as *www.lastminute.com*, *www.ebookers.com* or *www.expedia.com* for routes and fares.

There are also over 30 direct charter flights a week from airports around the UK to Menorca throughout the summer with services running from April to October for terms of one or two weeks. Contact the major package tourist companies such as **Thomas Cook** (*tel in the UK: 0870 750 5711; www.thomascook.co.uk*) for more details. **First Choice** flies charter flights from nine British airports, including Bristol and Gatwick (*www.firstchoice.co.uk*). **Thomson** also flies charter from Birmingham, Manchester, Cardiff and Edinburgh (*www.thomson.co.uk*). These companies sell holiday packages (flight and accommodation) but also sell flight-only tickets if you want to arrange your own accommodation.

Arriving by sea

Acciona Trasmediterránea (*www.trasmediterranea.es*) and **Balearia**

An inter-island ferry

(*www.balearia.net*) both operate vehicle and passenger ferry services from the Spanish mainland to Maó. There are ferry services from Maó and Ciutadella to Alcúdia on Mallorca. Details and times of ferry services may be found in the *Thomas Cook European Rail Timetable*, which is available to buy online from *www.thomascook publishing.com*, from branches of Thomas Cook in the UK or by telephoning *01733 416477*.

Camping

There are large campsites at **Tori Soli Nou** near Son Bou (*tel: 971 37 26 05; www.campingsonbou.com; open: May–Oct*) and in the hills above **Cala Galdana** (*Camping S'Atalaia; tel: 971 37 30 95; www.campingsatalaia.com; open: May–Oct*).

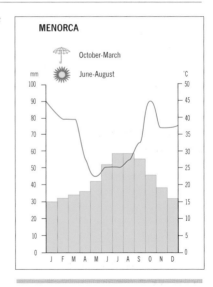

WEATHER CONVERSION CHART

25.4mm = 1 inch

°F = 1.8 × °C + 32

Climate

Menorca has a Mediterranean maritime climate with hot, dry summers and mild winters. The bulk of rainfall takes place between October and December, although thunderstorms are frequent in summer.

Crime

When you visit Menorca you will be at a relatively low risk of being a victim of serious crime; however, petty crime such as theft and pickpocketing can be a problem, especially from vehicles. It pays to take precautions to minimise your chances of a loss.

- Do not leave valuables in a car and leave nothing at all on show.
- Don't carry large amounts of cash or valuables with you.
- Deposit valuables in the hotel safe.
- Take extra care at cashpoint machines: don't allow bystanders to see your PIN (personal identification number).
- Put all money away before you leave banks or bureau de change kiosks.
- Don't leave valuables unattended in cafés, bars and restaurants.

Customs regulations

The following duty-free rules apply for visitors arriving from outside the EU:

- 200 cigarettes or 250g tobacco
- 1 litre of spirits or 2 litres of fortified or sparkling wine
- 2 litres of table wine
- 60ml of perfume
- 250ml of toilet water
- £145 worth of goods and souvenirs

There are no currency restrictions. Usual customs regulations apply for travellers arriving from other EU countries.

Driving

General rules: drive on the right and pass on the left. Most main roads have good surfaces. Minor roads may be uneven and narrow with limited vision, blind bends and hidden entrances. Road signs and markings comply with the European standard. Alcohol limits are 0.5mg per 100ml of blood. Children should be seated in the back in child seats. Seat belts must be worn by all passengers, and speaking on mobile phones while driving is prohibited. When a Spanish motorist flashes oncoming traffic, it is not a signal for you to proceed. It is a signal that they are coming through.

Bringing your own vehicle

Carry the registration document, valid insurance and your licence at all times. It is compulsory to carry a high-visibility jacket and two warning triangles in case of accident or breakdown – put your jacket on and place the cones some distance in front of and behind the car.

Car rental

If you are hiring a car, you will need both parts of your UK driving licence with you. Most car hire companies accept a regular driver's licence if you're from the EU, US, Canada, Australia or

New Zealand. If you are coming from outside these areas or from Iceland, Norway, Switzerland and Liechtenstein, you will need an International Driver's Licence. You have to be 21 to hire a car and a credit card imprint is required when picking up the car. There are car hire offices in all the main resorts and at the airport in the Arrivals Hall.

Fuel

There are several petrol stations around Maó and Ciutadella, and along the main road between the two, but there are few on the rest of the island so keep the tank topped up. Most petrol stations are open 7am–9pm and a few are open 24 hours. Most of the others have self-service machines outside these hours where you can pay for your petrol in advance using euro notes or credit cards. All hire cars take the unleaded (*sin plomo*) petrol Eurosuper.

Parking

Car parks and most street parking are pay zones – look for blue marking on the surface. Payment is normally 9.30am–1.30pm and 5–9pm (be aware that this is different to the UK, with parking tickets required well into the evening), but local regulations may vary so check the machine. Keep small change for meters. Your best bet in Maó is to use the underground car parks under Plaça de S'Esplanada or along Es Cos de Gràcia. In Ciutadella, make sure you use a meter on Avinguda Jaume I El Conquistador, and keep an

CONVERSION TABLE

FROM	TO	MULTIPLY BY
Inches	Centimetres	2.54
Feet	Metres	0.3048
Yards	Metres	0.9144
Miles	Kilometres	1.6090
Acres	Hectares	0.4047
Gallons	Litres	4.5460
Ounces	Grams	28.35
Pounds	Grams	453.6
Pounds	Kilograms	0.4536
Tons	Tonnes	1.0160

To convert back, for example from centimetres to inches, divide by the number in the third column.

eye on the time – those traffic wardens don't miss a trick.

Speed limits

Rural lanes – 30kph (19mph)
Urban/villages – 50kph (31mph)
All other roads – 90kph (56mph)
Specific limits may apply in towns – always keep an eye on speed signs. The police are very keen – if you are speeding they will get you and you will incur an on-the-spot fine!

Cycling

Cycling is very popular on Menorca and is both a flexible and inexpensive way of seeing the island and getting off the beaten track. If you are planning on bringing your own bicycle, check with the airline first as some budget airlines may charge a substantial sum if you are over the deemed allowance. Alternatively, renting a bicycle is straightforward and there are numerous outlets. The local

(*Cont. on p184*)

Language

Catalan is similar to Spanish (*Castellano*), but it is definitely a language of its own with its own peculiarities. Like English, Catalan uses the unstressed 'uh' sound that appears in nearly every multi-syllable word. Thus 'How are you?', which is '¿Cómo estás?' in Spanish, with every vowel pronouned, becomes '¿Com estàs?' in Catalan, with the first vowel in 'estàs' being an unstressed 'uh' sound. Consonants coming at the end of a word are often unpronounced. For example, *senyor* ('sir') is pronounced Sen-yoh, with no 'r' sound. 'V' is pronounced like a 'B', so *vosté* (the formal 'you') sounds like Boo-steh.

BASIC WORDS AND PHRASES

	CATALAN	SPANISH (CASTILIAN)
Hello	Hola	Hola
Goodbye	Adéu	Adiós
Yes	Si	Sí
No	No	No
Please	Sisplau	Por favor
Thank you	Graciès	Gracias
You're welcome	De res	De nada
Do you speak English?	Vostè parla Angles?	Habla inglés?
I don't speak Catalan/Spanish	No parla Català	No hablo español
Good day	Bon dia	Buenos días
Goodnight	Bona nit	Buenas noches
Excuse me	Perdoni	Perdón
Sir	Senyor	Señor
Madam	Senyora	Señora
How are you?	Como està?	Cómo està?
Very well, than you	Molt bé, gràcies	Muy bien, gracias
My name is ...	Em dic...	Me llamo ...
What's your name?	Come et dius?	Cómo se llama Usted?
How do I get to ?	Per anar a ...?	Para ir a ....?
Where is ...?	On és ...?	Donde està ...?
The subway	El metro	El metro
The airport	L'aeroport	El aeropuerto
The train station	El estació de tren	La estación de tren
The bus	El bus	El bus
The street	El carrer	La calle
A taxi	Un taxi	Un taxi
A hotel	Un hotel	Un hotel
The bathroom	El lavabo	Los aseos
A pharmacy	Una farmàcia	Una farmàcia
A bank	Un banc	El banco
The tourist office	L'oficina de turisme	La oficina de turismo
What time is it?	Qina hora és?	Qué hora es?

EMERGENCIES

	CATALAN	SPANISH (CASTILIAN)
Help!	Socors!	Socorro!
I am sick	Em trobo malament	Estoy enfermo/a
I am hurt	Estic ferit/ferida	Estoy herido/a
Hospital	L'hospital	El hospital
A doctor	Un metge	Un médico

DAYS AND MONTHS

	CATALAN	SPANISH (CASTILIAN)
Monday	Dilluns	Lunes
Tuesday	Dimarts	Martes
Wednesday	Dimecres	Miércoles
Thursday	Dijous	Jueves
Friday	Divendres	Viernes
Saturday	Dissabte	Sábado
Sunday	Diumenge	Domingo
January	Gener	Enero
February	Febrer	Febrero
March	Març	Marzo
April	Abril	Abril
May	Maig	Mayo
June	Juny	Junio
July	Juliol	Julio
August	Agost	Agosto
September	Setembre	Septiembre
October	Octubre	Octubre
November	Novembre	Noviembre
December	Desembre	Diciembre

NUMBERS

	CATALAN	SPANISH (CASTILIAN)
Zero	Zero	Cero
One	Un/Una	Uno
Two	Dos/Dues	Dos
Three	Tres	Tres
Four	Quatre	Cuatro
Five	Cinc	Cinco
Six	Sis	Seis
Seven	Set	Siete
Eight	Vuit	Ocho
Nine	Nou	Nueve
Ten	Deu	Diez

tourist offices or your hotel can advise you. You can also contact the **Asociacíon Cicloturista de Menorca**, *tel: 971 36 48 16; www.ciclomenorca.com*

Electricity

Menorca's system is 220 volts with two-pin plugs. If you are travelling from the UK, you will need an adaptor plug. These are available in electrical shops or chemists.

Embassies and consulates

Menorca Honorary British Vice-Consulate *Sa Casa Nova, Camí de Biniatap 30, 07720 Es Castell. Tel: 971 36 33 73.*

All embassies are located in Madrid:

Australian Embassy *Plaza Descubridor Diego de Ordás 3, 28003 Madrid. Tel: 913 53 66 90. www.spain.embassy.gov.au*

Canadian Embassy *Goya Building, Núñez de Balbao 35, 28001 Madrid. Tel: 914 23 32 50. www.canada-es.org*

Republic of Ireland *Ireland House, Paseo de la Castellana 46–4, 28046 Madrid. Tel: 914 36 40 93.*

New Zealand *Pinar 7, 3rd floor, 28006 Madrid. Tel: 915 23 02 26. www.nzembassy.com*

South Africa *Calle de Claudio Coello 91–6, 28006 Madrid. Tel: 914 36 37 80. www.dfa.gov.za*

Police cars in Alaior

UK Embassy *Paseo de Recoletos 7/9,*
28004 Madrid. Tel: 915 24 97 00.
www.britishembassy.gov.uk
US Embassy *Calle Serrano 75, 28006*
Madrid. Tel: 915 87 22 00.
www.embusa.es

Emergency numbers

The pan-European emergency number
is *112* and is free from any phone line,
mobile or payphone.

Health

There are no compulsory inoculations
for travel to Menorca.

Medical provision is of a high standard
with some English-speaking medical
staff. The national health service has a
hospital in Maó (Verge del Toro) and
various outpatient surgeries spread out
through the island. There are also several
private medical centres on the island; the
local tourist office can provide you with a
list. The Red Cross is also present in the
main towns and beach resorts. In some
areas, there will be someone providing a
voluntary translation service to help with
doctor's appointments.

The water is drinkable but bottled
water tastes better.

Pharmacies (*farmacias*) sell many
drugs over the counter, but brand
names vary, so if you need a specific
medication or drug take an empty
packet with you to aid the pharmacist
or carry a prescription from your
doctor. Chemists in the pharmacies are
qualified to diagnose symptoms and
prescribe medicine in their own right.

Insurance

Having adequate health insurance
cover is vital. UK citizens with a
European Health Insurance Card
(EHIC) will be treated without charge,
but a travel insurance policy will also
cover repatriation if the injuries or
illness warrants it. The European
Health Insurance Card is available
online at *www.ehic.org.uk*, by phoning
0845 606 2030 or from post offices.
All other nationalities should ensure
adequate cover for illness, as they will
be charged at point of treatment.

If you have medical insurance or are
willing to pay for treatment, you can
contact one of the numerous private
clinics on the island. Your hotel or the
tourist office can provide you with a
list. Dental treatment is not generally
covered by insurance and, in an
emergency, you will be billed on
the spot.

Travellers should always have cover
for everything they carry with them in
case of loss or theft.

Insurance companies also usually
provide cover for cancellation of
holiday or travel delay in their policies.
Though not essential, this cover offers
some compensation if travel plans
go awry.

Internet access

A few cafés in Maó and Ciutadella have
Internet access, as do several in the
larger resorts. Most large hotels will
have Wi-Fi connections or some form
of Internet access.

Café Gelats Parpal

A bar-café incorporating an Internet café called World Next Door.
Carrer Hannover 21, Maó. Tel: 971 35 34 75. Open: daily 11am–10pm.

Tobogán

Buzzing pizzeria with Internet access.
Platja Cala Galdana, Cala Galdana. Tel: 971 15 46 16. Open: daily 9.30am–11.30pm.

Viva Menorca Apartments

Internet access.
Calle Llevant, Cala'n Bosch. Tel: 971 38 78 43. Open: daily 24 hours.

Lost property

You will need an official police report to make an insurance claim for any lost property. If you lose your passport, contact your embassy or consulate immediately.

Maps

Maó and Ciutadella tourist offices have maps of their respective towns. Basic touring maps can be picked up from the car rental companies, but for a detailed map try the Mapa Turístico (tourist map) E-54. It is reliable and (mostly) accurate and available from supermarkets all over the island.

Media

A good selection of English newspapers can be bought in the resorts, the more popular ones being printed in Spain. Many popular English magazines can be easily found in Menorca. The larger supermarkets have an excellent selection of newspapers and magazines for all ages. Most hotels have satellite TV so you can watch your favourite programmes in English. Most British-owned bars and restaurants also have satellite TV and usually organise a special night if there is an important event on TV including football!

Money matters

Money

The currency of Spain (Menorca) is the euro. One euro is made up of one hundred cents. Coins come in denominations of 1, 2, 5, 10, 20 and 50 cents, 1 and 2 euros. Notes are in denominations of 5, 10, 20, 50, 100 and 500 euros.

ATMs

ATMs are numerous and you will be able to get cash in the major towns. Be sure to contact your bank before you travel to let them know your plans. If not, you may be unable to withdraw funds.

Credit cards

Credit cards are widely accepted across Menorca. The most popular are MasterCard and Visa. You can also use your credit card to get cash advances over the counter in banks and from ATMs, although there will be a commission charge.

Currency exchange

Almost all banks in Menorca will exchange currency, and commission rates are generally low. Hotels, apartment complexes and commercial bureaux de change will also exchange but will charge a higher commission fee than a bank.

Traveller's cheques

Now losing popularity with the increase in ATMs and the use of credit cards abroad, these are still the safest way to carry holiday cash as they can be replaced if they are lost or stolen. You can change traveller's cheques at most large hotels or at bureaux de change and banks, but the same advice applies about the danger of high commission rates as with cash.

Opening hours

Shops: generally *Mon–Fri 9am–1pm & 5–8pm, Sat 9am–1pm.*
Supermarkets: *Mon–Sat 9am–8pm.*
Banks: *Mon–Fri 8.30am–2.15pm.*
Museums: have varying opening hours but mainly *Tue–Sat 9am–1pm & 4–8pm.* Hours are likely to be shorter in the winter months.

Pharmacies

There are duty pharmacies in all the major towns. A list of late openings can be found in most pharmacy windows.

Police

In an emergency, call *112.*
There are three separate police forces in Spain:
Guardia Civil: riot and crowd control, highways and non-urban areas; green uniforms. *Tel: 062.*

Policía Nacional: for reporting theft or lost items; brown uniforms. *Tel: 091.*
Policía Municipal: local town police; blue uniforms. *Tel: 092.*

Post offices

Post offices (*correus*) can be found in all major towns and the service is reliable.
Maó *Open: Mon–Fri 9am–9pm, Sat 9am–2pm.*
Ciutadella *Open: Mon–Fri 9am–7pm, Sat 9am–2pm.*
Post offices in other towns may have odd opening hours but will largely follow the ones given above.
Most shops selling postcards will also sell stamps (*segells*). Postboxes are bright yellow.

Public holidays

The following dates are official holidays in Spain – some dates can move so check with the tourist office. All government buildings, banks and most commercial businesses will be closed but main holiday resorts will operate as usual.

1 January Cap d'Any (New Year's Day)
6 January Día des Reis (Epiphany)
19 March Sant Josep (St Joseph's Day)
March/April Dijous Sant (Maundy Thursday)
March/April Divendres Sant (Good Friday)
March/April Pasqua Florida (Easter Monday)
1 May Festa del Treball (Labour Day)
Early June Dilluns de Pasqua Granada (Whit Monday)

24 June Sant Joan (St John's Day)
29 June Sant Pere I Sant Pau (St Peter and St Paul's Day)
25 July Santiago (St James's Day)
15 August Assumpcío (Assumption Day)
12 October Día de la Hispanitat (Spanish National Day)
1 November Tots Sants (All Saints' Day)
6 December Día de la Constitució (Constitution Day)
8 December Imaculada (Immaculate Conception)
25 December Nadal (Christmas Day)
26 December Sant Esteve (St Stephen's Day)

Public transport
Bus
There is a bus service running from Maó and linking all the major towns of the centre to Ciutadella across the spine of the island. Timetables are available at tourist offices and hotels or apartment complexes. You can buy tickets from the driver as you enter the bus.

Transports de les Illes Balears runs services across the island but three different companies fulfil the contracts. **Transportes Menorca** or **TMSA** (*tel: 971 38 03 93; www.tmsa.es*) run services from Maó to Ciutadella, Es Castell, Punta Prima, Binibeca, Cala'n Porter, Son Bou, Sant Tomàs and Cala Galdana.

Autocares Fornells (*tel: 971 15 43 90; www.autosfornells.com*) connects Fornells with Maó via Arenal d'en Castell, Son Parc and Es Grau.

Autocares Torres (*tel: 971 38 64 61; www.e-torres.net*) connects Ciutadella with Cala'n Bosch, Cala Blanca, Cala'n Blanes, Cala'n Forcat and Cala Morell.

Sustainable tourism
Thomas Cook is a strong advocate of ethical and fairly traded tourism and believes that the travel experience should be as good for the places visited as it is for the people who visit them. That's why we're a firm supporter of The Travel Foundation: a charity that develops solutions to help improve and protect holiday destinations, their environment, traditions and culture. To find out what you can do to make a positive difference to the places you travel to and the people who live there, please visit *www.makeholidaysgreener.org.uk*

Telephones
Modern hotels will usually have a direct-dial phone system, but they often charge extortionate surcharges for calls. Ask about charges before you make the decision to ring home – it may be cheaper to use your mobile.

The country code for Menorca (Spain) is *(00) 34*. Menorcan numbers have nine digits.

Telephoning abroad
Australia *00* + *61* + area code (minus the 0) + telephone number
New Zealand *00 64* + area code (minus the 0) + telephone number
Republic of Ireland *00 353* + area code (minus the 0) + telephone number

South Africa *00 27* + area code (minus the 0) + telephone number
UK *00 44* + area code (minus the 0) + telephone number
United States and Canada *00 1* + area code (minus the 0) + telephone number.

Public phones are now almost 100 per cent card (credit card or phonecard) operated. You can buy phonecards from news kiosks and tobacconists (*tabacs*). Mobile (cell) phone coverage is good in the main towns and along main highways. Check with your mobile phone company for details (cost and partner provision) of their service on Menorca.

Time
Menorca works to Central European Time, which is 1 hour ahead of Greenwich Mean Time in winter and 2 hours ahead in summer. If it is 1pm in Maó, it is noon in London.

Menorca is 6 hours ahead of Washington DC and 9 hours ahead of Los Angeles in the US. The island is 6 hours behind Toronto and 9 hours behind Vancouver in Canada. In Australia, Perth is 7 hours ahead of Menorca and Sydney 10. Auckland in New Zealand is 12 hours ahead of Menorca.

Tipping
Tipping is not expected in restaurants where service is already added to the bill. If not, a 10–15 per cent tip should be added. In bars and cafés it is customary to leave small change. Always tip bellboys and room cleaners.

Toilets
Lavatories are generally of a good standard but there are few public facilities. The best policy is to use the facilities of a café or bar, but you should buy a drink if you do.

Tourist information
There are tourist information offices on the island at the following locations:
The arrivals hall at Maó airport.
Tel: 971 15 71 15.
Moll de Llevant 2, Maó.
Tel: 971 35 59 52.
Plaça de la Catedral, Ciutadella.
Tel: 971 38 26 93.

The following websites are also useful:
www.gocatalunya.com
www.menorca.es

Travellers with disabilities
Provision for travellers with mobility problems is variable. New buildings have to meet a code standard for wheelchair access and some are adapted. Always make specific enquiries with hotels if you require specially equipped rooms. By the very nature of its natural attractions, some areas will be difficult to access.

For more holiday information for people with disabilities, contact Holiday Care Services. *Tel (UK): 0845 124 9971. www.tourismforall.org.uk*

Index

Acknowledgements

Thomas Cook Publishing wishes to thank PETE BENNETT, BIG WORLD PRODUCTIONS, to whom the copyright belongs, for the photographs in this book, except for the following images:

BINIARROCA HOTEL RURAL 177
DREAMSTIME 1, 143 (Quintanilla), 27 (Caravan), 91 (Tonystrange11)
SASHA HESELTINE 9, 19, 21, 23, 31, 38, 44, 46, 47, 53, 59, 71, 72, 83, 84, 86, 109, 113, 121, 122, 124, 125, 127, 132, 139, 147, 149, 151, 153, 159, 160, 165, 166, 168, 175, 184
SET HOTELS 176
THOMAS COOK PUBLISHING 51, 103, 128, 162
TIM NEWTON 172
WIKIMEDIA COMMONS 24 (Gabino Bolívar Subirats), 29 (1997), 110 (mac 9), 167 (Calibas)
WORLD PICTURES/PHOTOSHOT 33, 77

For CAMBRIDGE PUBLISHING MANAGEMENT LIMITED:
Project editor: Ed Robinson
Typesetter: Paul Queripel
Proofreaders: Jan McCann & Caroline Hunt

SEND YOUR THOUGHTS TO
BOOKS@THOMASCOOK.COM

We're committed to providing the very best up-to-date information in our travel guides and constantly strive to make them as useful as they can be. You can help us to improve future editions by letting us have your feedback. If you've made a wonderful discovery on your travels that we don't already feature, if you'd like to inform us about recent changes to anything that we do include, or if you simply want to let us know your thoughts about this guidebook and how we can make it even better – we'd love to hear from you.

Send us ideas, discoveries and recommendations today and then look out for your valuable input in the next edition of this title.

Emails to the above address, or letters to the traveller guides Series Editor, Thomas Cook Publishing, PO Box 227, Coningsby Road, Peterborough PE3 8SB, UK.

Please don't forget to let us know which title your feedback refers to!